So You Want to…

Be a

REAL ESTATE AGENT

How to Pass Your State License Exam

By Angela Erickson

SO YOU WANT TO... BE A REAL ESTATE AGENT: HOW TO PASS YOUR STATE LICENSE EXAM

1405 SW 6th Avenue • Ocala, Florida 34471 • Phone 800-814-1132 • Fax 352-622-1875
Website: www.atlantic-pub.com • Email: sales@atlantic-pub.com
SAN Number: 268-1250

Library of Congress Cataloging-in-Publication Data

Names: Erickson, Angela, author.
Title: So you want to— be a real estate agent : how to pass your state license exam / by Angela Erickson.
Description: Ocala : Atlantic Publishing Group, Inc, [2017] | Includes bibliographical references and index.
Identifiers: LCCN 2017027813 (print) | LCCN 2017044596 (ebook) | ISBN 9781620232125 (ebook) | ISBN 9781620232118 (alk. paper) | ISBN 1620232111 (alk. paper)
Subjects: LCSH: Real estate agents. | Real estate business.
Classification: LCC HD1382 (ebook) | LCC HD1382 .E75 2017 (print) | DDC 333.33076—dc23
LC record available at https://lccn.loc.gov/2017027813

Printed in the United States

INTERIOR LAYOUT: Nicole Sturk

Reduce. Reuse.
RECYCLE.

A decade ago, Atlantic Publishing signed the Green Press Initiative. These guidelines promote environmentally friendly practices, such as using recycled stock and vegetable-based inks, avoiding waste, choosing energy-efficient resources, and promoting a no-pulping policy. We now use 100-percent recycled stock on all our books. The results: in one year, switching to post-consumer recycled stock saved 24 mature trees, 5,000 gallons of water, the equivalent of the total energy used for one home in a year, and the equivalent of the greenhouse gases from one car driven for a year.

Over the years, we have adopted a number of dogs from rescues and shelters. First there was Bear and after he passed, Ginger and Scout. Now, we have Kira, another rescue. They have brought immense joy and love not just into our lives, but into the lives of all who met them.

We want you to know a portion of the profits of this book will be donated in Bear, Ginger and Scout's memory to local animal shelters, parks, conservation organizations, and other individuals and nonprofit organizations in need of assistance.

– Douglas & Sherri Brown,
President & Vice-President of Atlantic Publishing

TABLE OF CONTENTS

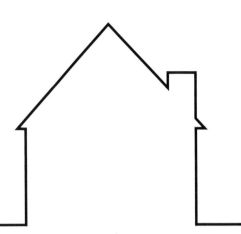

INTRODUCTION

DO I WANT TO BE
A REALTOR?

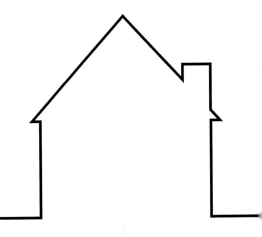

SO, YOU'RE THINKING ABOUT BECOMING A REALTOR. CON-grats! Real estate is an exciting career. Helping someone find the home of his or her dreams is rewarding, and getting to see gorgeous houses — or imagining the potential shown by a fixer-upper — might sound like a dream job to you. However, there are some steps to take before you can officially call yourself a Realtor — preparing for the licensing exam is your first step toward reaching your goals.

In all 50 states (plus Washington D.C.), a real estate agent must have a license before helping sell or buy a house. And each state might have different laws about the real estate license.

HOW DID THE REAL ESTATE PROFESSION START?

Before the American Revolution, most people in Europe lived in what we call the feudal system: the king owned all the land. He divided it into pieces called *feuds*, and then gave land to the lords who were faithful to him. In turn, these lords subleased parts of the land to "subjects" around them. (That's where we get the term "landlord.")

By the time of the Revolutionary War, the American colonists wanted a different way of living. A relatively new idea was for individuals to own the land. Enter the "American Dream." The United States Constitution and Bill of Rights supported the individual's right to own property. These important documents became the foundation of later licensing laws that govern today's real estate profession.

A profession is born

Early in our nation's history, people lived in small communities, and people knew when someone bought property from someone else. By the late 1800s, American society had changed — the population had grown considerably, and people began to move around to find new opportunities.

As a result, more real estate was bought and sold, but now the buyers and sellers did not know one another, so they needed a person they could trust to handle the business. They needed a trusted agent who knew the property. Eventually, the job of real estate professional emerged.

THE HOMESTEAD ACT

In 1862, this new law let people own land in exchange for improving and developing the land for at least five years. The U.S. government gave out more than 300 million acres of public property to private landowners.

So, how did licensing of real estate agents begin?

In 1908, the National Association of REALTORS® (NAR) was founded to help set standards and make the profession seem more legitimate. By 1963, all 50 states and the District of Columbia required salespeople and brokers to be licensed.

Although the real estate market took a severe downturn in the mid-2000s, the market has since rebounded. In 2014, real estate construction alone contributed nearly $1.1 trillion — more than 6.1 percent — to the nation's economic output as measured by Gross Domestic Product.

> **Words of Wisdom:** The reason why I got into real estate is because I wanted to become my own boss. I had worked at the corporate level and at the small business level with my family. Having your own business has it pluses. For me, the experience I had prior to getting my license helped me once I got my license. I have always treated my profession as a full time job because that is what it is, a full time job with full time responsibilities. Too many people get into our business for the wrong reason and do not treat it like a full time job and full time responsibility. – Mark Hampton, Licensed REALTOR® in Texas

READY TO MOVE FORWARD?

Although this is a brief history, it will help you realize that you are heading off on a noble and rewarding profession.

Now that you know some real estate history, you can begin the first step in your career: learning how to prepare for your examination.

CHAPTER 1
PREPARING FOR YOUR EXAM

DID WE SAY EXAM? DON'T FREAK OUT.

And don't freak out if you hear the (true) fact that in the last few years, only around half of those who took the real estate licensing examination actually passed the test the first time. By reading this book and beginning the process of preparing, you're already a step ahead!

The first step is to find out what your home state's licensing requirements are, because every state is different. Go to the back of this book and check out the Appendix — we've listed information for all 50 states.

EXAMS

You need a license in every state to sell real estate. Every state has its own rules, methods of testing, test versions, how old you should be to take the exam, rules about citizenship, how to apply, and rules about criminal background checks. For example, some states will make you take classes before getting licensed, and some states will allow you to take the test after you register — no pre-licensing classes needed.

Your state will either create its own tests or contract with one of these four standardized testing services.

- Applied Measurement Professionals

- Prometric

- Pearson Vue

- Psychological Services, Inc.

Contact information for these services are in the back of the book.

The difference between the tests is how many questions are given for each topic. Keep in mind that you will also need to know your state's specific real estate laws to pass.

Get in contact with your state to find out what type of test you are required to take. If your state is contracted with one of these testing companies, call them to receive their information.

If you live in a state where you have to take certain classes before taking the licensing exam, your instructors should know this information and will be able to guide you.

STATE QUESTIONS

When you get in touch with the examination organization in your state, here are questions you need to ask to be prepared for the test:

- **What are the requirements to become a licensed real estate agent in my state?**
- **Which exam is given in my state?**
- **What topics are covered on the exam?**
- **How much does the test cost?**
- **How do I register for the exam?**
- **How much time am I given to take the exam?**
- **How is the exam scored?**
- **What is the passing score?**
- **Am I penalized for wrong answers?**
- **Is the exam on a computer or is it handwritten?**
- **What can I bring with me when I take the test?**
- **How do I make arrangements for special needs? (For example, handicapped accessibility or medical needs)**
- **Where and when is the exam given?**
- **If allowed, what type of calculator may I use?**
- **When will I get my score?**
- **What are the state-specific topics covered on the exam?**

- **What is the format of the test? Multiple-choice? True/False? Fill-in-the blank? Essay?**

- **Is there anything else I need to know?**

TESTING FORMATS

The test is broken into two parts: the first section is general in nature, and the second part is state-specific, covering your state's license laws.

The examination might include multiple-choice, true or false, fill-in-the-blank, and short-answer questions. However, most states give only multiple-choice exams.

All tests are timed, lasting anywhere between three to five hours depending on the state. We'll talk later on about making the most of your time in your examination.

Another difference between the states is what a passing score means. Also, some states penalize you for a wrong answer. If not, then it will become important for you to guess at the answer. Later, we will discuss test-taking strategies, such as how to guess through the process of elimination.

The key to passing your real estate exam will be to study the materials and master them, no matter what type of test you take.

REAL ESTATE AGENT VS. BROKER

You've probably heard both terms: agent and broker. The difference is basically based on the legal definitions, which are different in each state.

The difference between a real estate agent and a broker is the level of experience and education. For example, in most states, you have to become a licensed salesperson first and work in this area before you are allowed to become a broker. A broker can work alone and would be able to hire agents under himself or herself. Most states also require a broker to have more educational and professional development classes before he or she can get a broker license.

BUT, in certain states (like Colorado), all of their real estate licensees are under one status called "Brokers." (Check with your state to see how they handle agent and broker titles!)

WHAT IS A REALTOR®?

A REALTOR® is the professional name given to the licensed agent by the National Association of Realtors when an agent becomes a member of the group. A REALTOR® must live by a strict code of ethics and is committed to the real estate profession.

Not all licensed agents are REALTORS®, but every REALTOR® is a licensed agent. This title is over and above the existing requirements, and some brokers require their agents to become a member of this professional trade group.

 To find out more information, visit www.realtor.org.

WHAT TO TAKE TO YOUR EXAM

Each state has different ways to register, so make sure you read and follow them carefully. For example, some states require a broker to sign your application form. Usually, you send in an application and a fee to take the test. Your state will then send back an entry permit into the examination. The information will include where and when you will be taking the exam.

Check with your state agency about what is allowed into your test-taking area. Find out all procedures so you are as well prepared as possible, and also remember to find out if you are allowed to use a calculator in the exam and, if so, what type. Graphing calculators, smartphones, and tablets are often restricted.

GETTING READY FOR THE EXAM

Yup, you're going to have to study. You can't go into a real estate exam, even after taking the pre-licensing courses, and expect to pass the exam without spending some time studying. The tests are too difficult, and some questions are designed to confuse you. The examinations are to see how well you understand the many areas of real estate.

The best way to start studying is to make a plan. It is a good idea to think about how much time you actually need to study before registering for the exam. Do you need 30 days, 45 days, or can you master the materials in 10 days? Determining how much time you may need is a personal choice.

One of the keys to passing your real estate test will be to take the exam when you're at your peak knowledge performance. In other words, when you know as much as you can know about all the topics and feel confident in your ability, take the exam.

Most experts agree that you should study every day for at least 20 minutes to avoid getting overwhelmed.

HELP! I HAVE TEST ANXIETY!

The number one tip to get rid of test anxiety is to be prepared. When you know your information and what to expect, you will feel empowered, and this will help you pass the exam.

Pay attention to how you're thinking and feeling. Having a positive attitude really does make a difference!

Be active as well. Studies show that physical activity helps focus your mind and increases certain chemicals in the brain known to improve your mood. If you are currently on an exercise schedule, do not quit now; keep it up. If you aren't doing any physical activity right now, it's a good time to add some to your day.

TEST-TAKING STRATEGIES

A few days before the exam, make a trial run to the location of the test. If you need to make changes to your directions, make them before test day. Use an app or GPS to get traffic conditions ahead of time.

Try not to study the day or night before the exam. By this time, you should have prepared enough that you don't need another full day of studying. Try to do something fun to take your mind off of the exam.

The night before the exam, make sure you set out everything that you need to take with you the next day. You will need the following, including anything else your state agency tells you to bring:

- Registration/Entrance ticket to the exam

- Calculator

- Photo ID (you may need two forms)

- No. 2 pencils

- Watch

- Sweater or jacket (you never know the temperature in the exam room)

Get plenty of sleep the night before the exam. A well-rested mind and body will boost your stamina for the test. Allow enough time in the morning for a good breakfast of both carbohydrates and proteins. Studies show that this improves your brain performance. Your mom was right — eat your breakfast!

ARRIVING AT THE EXAM

You will want to arrive to your test site at least 30 minutes before the exam. Arriving early means you will have enough time to use the restroom, keep yourself calm, and find your examination room. Take some deep breaths, tell yourself that you will pass, and get started!

Make sure you understand all the rules for the examination. If you have any questions, ask the person giving the test.

HOW TO DOMINATE AT THE REAL ESTATE EXAM

The key to kicking the exam's butt is time management.

Here are some other important tips:

Food and water

To get your body ready for a long exam like this one, you should be nourished. Fuel your brain! Health.com suggests the following foods as natural concentration boosters for the brain: dark chocolate, blueberries, salmon, green tea, beets, bananas, spinach, and eggs. Also, drink plenty of water and, if you're allowed, bring a water bottle into the testing room. Being hydrated helps while taking a long exam.

Follow directions

It sounds simple, but you want to read over all the directions in each section to make sure that you understand them.

Read every word

Make sure you read every word in every question and answer, but read them quickly. It is extremely important that you keep the correct pace but not at the expense of missing key parts of the questions.

Keep moving

If you don't know the answer to a question, skip it and come back to it later. Make sure that you remember the ones you skipped, so you can find it easily.

Use scrap paper to its full advantage

If you are allowed scrap paper, quickly jot down definitions and math formulas on it.

Don't rush

Rushing leads to panic. Instead, work at a steady pace so you can remain calm throughout the test.

Learn the process of elimination

When you come to a question, and you are not sure of the answer, mark off the one or two answers that you know are wrong. Then, think through the answers that are left to choose the one that you feel answers the question best. If you cannot decide on a definite answer, you have two options: skip the question and come back to it, or go ahead and guess (especially if you are pressed for time and there is no penalty for guessing). You can also try this two-step strategy:

Step 1: Eliminate the most unlikely answers first. Doing so will increase your odds of choosing the right answer every time.

Step 2: Use your gut feeling to make a quick guess. Don't dwell too long on a difficult question; rely on your gut feeling.

Don't overanalyze

Usually, the first answer that comes to you is the correct one. Part of the problem with overanalyzing is that you start to second-guess yourself. If you are well prepared, you will tend to recognize the correct answer immediately.

Change answers

This might seem like it goes against the last tip, but there will be times when it makes sense to change your answers. As you go through the test, one question might jog your memory or help answer an earlier question.

Be prepared for math questions

About 10 percent of the real estate exam has to do with math. Test-takers need skills in arithmetic, geometry, algebra, and word problems. Chapter 6 will focus on how to solve sample math problems covered on the licensing exam.

Cramming

"Cramming" is when one studies super hard right before the day of testing. We don't recommend this. Skimming through and reviewing the more difficult concepts is time well spent. The studying process should be planned in plenty of time and allow for the unexpected.

You'll be surprised at how much you know when taking the exam, so work through all questions at a steady and even pace. Skip questions you don't know or that will take more time to figure out, and come back to them after you have completed the easier questions.

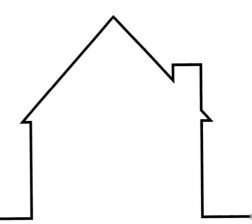

CHAPTER 2
REAL ESTATE PRACTICES AND PRINCIPLES

THIS CHAPTER TALKS ABOUT THE TYPICAL REAL ESTATE PRAC-
tices and principles that you need to know as a real estate sales agent.

REAL VS. PERSONAL PROPERTY

Real property means the land plus all the buildings and improvements made to the land — including all the rights. These rights include *subsurface rights*, but may or may not include *air rights*. Air rights mean the area right above the property lining up into the atmosphere — where a plane would fly. Improvements would include all buildings and structures, as well as utilities and other site and landscape improvements that make the property efficient and look nice. The buildings do not have to be living space; garages and sheds are also improvements.

Real property is divided into *corporeal* and *incorporeal*. Corporeal means all of the tangible rights, such as building or utility improvements (items that you can touch and feel). Incorporeal property would be considered intangible and includes things like rights of way or easements.

Personal property is anything that's *not* real property, or what we listed above. This can also be called "personalty" or "chattel" and can include anything that moves, like lawnmowers, furniture, clothing, televisions, and the like. Personal property is anything that is not attached to the real property. In a property sale, items like plumbing fixtures, cabinets, and doors are considered real property, as they are actually attached to the home.

In some cases, people might disagree on what is truly real property, and those details should be listed in writing in the Purchase and Sale Agreement. Stoves and dishwashers are nearly always considered real property as they are permanently piped, drained, and/or wired to the building (not just plugged in like a refrigerator). If you're trying to figure out whether an item is personal or real property, ask yourself: is it portable?

Emblements (or *fructus industriales*) are also considered personal property. This means crops grown on a property and cared for by the person living at the property.

Fixtures are one group of items that consistently become a matter of interpretation. Personal property that over time becomes real property is called a "fixture." When an item changes from real to personal property, we call that *severance*. An owner could do this by cutting down a tree in order to sell the firewood or bark mulch.

To figure out whether an item is a fixture or not, think about the following:

1. **Intent of the parties**: If you have a 30-unit apartment building, you would expect the window air-conditioning units to stay with the property, but not in a single-family home.

2. **Method of annexation**: Can the fixture be easily removed, without a skilled professional/contractor, and without a large amount of time and effort?

3. **Agreement of the parties**: This should always be in writing, and should be listed as part of the Purchase and Sale Agreement.

A *trade fixture* is normally personal property that doesn't stay with the real estate during a sale, because this fixture is specifically used for business purposes. An example would be display cases in a jewelry store.

Real property's physical characteristics

Land is immobile: One can't take a piece of land and move it somewhere else.

Land is indestructible: One can change the surface or destroy the buildings on the land, but the property itself will never go away.

Land is unique: When all factors are considered, absolutely no two pieces of land are identical. This is important when considering the value of a property.

Real property's economic characteristics

Improvements: When you increase or change the use of the land, like roads, utilities, or buildings.

Scarcity: Also known as typical supply and demand. As a certain type of property becomes less available, its value goes up.

Long-term investment: Real estate is what we call a "fixed" entity or investment, because in many cases a property holding will be for decades. This is super important — especially when you talk about financing and interest charges. After the entire mortgage debt is paid off (which could be 20 to 30 years), the buyer then owns the property completely.

What does equity of redemption mean? In the past, if a borrower achieved *equity of redemption*, it meant he or she has the right to get back his or her property once the debt secured by the mortgage has been settled. The "equity of redemption" was the right to ask the courts of equity to transfer the property officially to the borrower.

Location: Everyone has heard the old real estate saying, "location, location, location." Of all the characteristics mentioned, it's clear that a property's exact location is the most important when determining value.

Property (or legal) rights

You have five basic legal rights when you own a piece of property:

1. *Exclusion*: to limit who comes onto your property

2. *Disposition*: to sell, transfer, or put the property in your will

3. *Enjoyment*: to use without others trespassing on your property rights

4. *Possession*: to hold and use (or not)

5. *Control*: to use the property however you want (within the law)

However, there are some limits to these rights.

Rights of Other Persons generally refers to the fact that your neighbors have a right to *quiet enjoyment* of their own property. To know these rights, you might have to do some research on the area's noise ordinance.

Property owners also need to think about these five ways their rights are not protected:

1. *Escheat:* This doesn't happen often, but if an owner dies without a will and there aren't any known survivors to inherit the property, the state will then own it. This is called *intestate succession.*

2. *Taxation:* Cities, towns, and counties get funds for their programs mostly through property taxes on home properties. If an owner doesn't pay their taxes, the town could seize the property.

 The city or town has the right to tax the property owner — it's called "Ad Valorem Taxation."

3. *Building Code:* Any structures built on the land have to follow the city or state building codes. Many older buildings and homes were built before there were any building codes, so the permission to use and live in them is called "being grandfathered" in. However, if any work was to be done on the home, including plumbing and electrical work, all the new work has to follow the local building codes. The health code (water and sewage) is usually part of the building department.

4. *Zoning Ordinance:* Also called zoning, this means community planning; it happens in most regions.

5. *Police Power:* Police need to enforce the laws of the community, so sometimes they will have to act on a willful denial of a building code or zoning violation as described above.

Land descriptions

When you're talking about buildable, empty lots, listings of land and lots will usually be described by to their characteristics, like rolling, wooded (heavily or sparsely), steep-grade, flat, wetland, well-draining, pastureland, or farmland.

When there's a specific place where something exists, the term for that place is called a *situs*.

Appraisers, along with developers and real estate investors, will need to analyze the land carefully to find its market value. A potential buyer will ask the following questions:

- Has a perc (percolation) test been done?

- Is there an approved septic design?

- Is the lot on town water and/or sewer service?

- Is there a private well on site? Drilled or dug well?

- Have soil borings been completed?

- Have test pits been dug?

- Have wetlands onsite been marked and delineated?

- Is there ledge at or just below the surfaces?

These and other questions may come up, and if you as the real estate agent don't know the answers, contact your broker or the seller directly.

CONTRACTS AND DEEDS

Contracts: To say it simply, a contract means two parties agree to do something. If one of the parties doesn't keep up their end, the other can take them to court. A real estate Purchase and Sale Agreement or an Offer to Purchase form is a type of written contract.

Some examples and brief definitions in the real estate arena are:

Listing Agreement: A contract between a seller and a real estate firm to sell a property.

Purchase and Sale Agreement: A contract between a buyer and a seller to buy a piece of property.

Buyer Agency Agreement: A contract between a buyer and a real estate firm to help the buyer purchase a property.

Lease: A landlord and a tenant agree on the rental of a property for a certain amount of money and time, with rules.

Deed: Gives the title to a piece of property — *also referred to as a title deed.*

Mortgage Note and Mortgage Deed: You need mortgages any time financing is done to buy real estate. A mortgage is a promise to pay, and the mortgage deed takes care of the details happening between the bank and the buyer before the loan is repaid in full.

Option: One side has the option to do or not do something within a certain time.

Right of First Refusal: Like an option, but here a price usually isn't listed. An example is that a tenant might have a right of first refusal to match any offer if the landlord wants to sell the property.

General contract classifications and elements

You won't be able to memorize all of these contract terms right away. That is better left to the real estate attorneys that you will be working for. However, here are some basics you should know:

Acceptance: Once an offer is accepted fully and the one making the offer— the offerer — knows this, the offer legally becomes a contract and is no longer an offer.

Expressed vs. Implied: Expressed means very specific. Implied means the specifics in a contract aren't listed, in writing or verbally.

Bilateral vs. Unilateral: Bilateral means each person must do something for the other person. A purchase and sale agreement is a bilateral contract. A unilateral contract is one where one party agrees to do something if the other party does something.

Executed vs. Executory: An executed contract means both parties have finished everything that each has agreed to do. In an executory contract, some or all of the steps have not been completed.

Consideration: A sale might not always be with money, but it does usually take something tangible. Sometimes someone will make a trade for another piece of real estate or an asset like a sailboat or yacht. This can happen if the sale isn't done at the exact contract time. For example, a buyer may say that he'll pay the full listing price over the course of 10 years (an example of seller financing), or the buyer will let the seller have complete use of his Aruba timeshare for the next three years.

Offer and Acceptance: Everyone has to agree to every part of a contract for it to be valid. The accepted offer must be communicated between everyone to make a binding contract.

 The person making the offer (which is not always the buyer) is the *offeror*, and the person receiving the offer is the *offeree*.

Competency: Both parties must be competent to sign a contract. This means being old enough, as well as having the mental status, ability, and emotional condition to sign the contract.

Consent: Everyone is acting out of his or her own free will to sign the contract — nobody is being forced into it.

WHAT COULD STOP A CONTRACT FROM GOING THROUGH?

You can't enforce a contract if these things happen:

Statute of Limitations: If everything listed in the contract isn't done by a certain date, the contract is void.

Laches: This means the time limit is not set specifically in the contract, but is still enforced if things aren't done in a "reasonable" period of time.

Estoppel: If some charge in the sale was later found to be wrong, the new owner can't be forced into paying it.

In real estate, many offers for a property will be presented and then will consequently not be accepted or the time limit may run out. Here are some other reasons for an offer to be terminated legally:

Death of Offeror: If the offeror dies before the offer is accepted and communicated back to him or her, the offer ceases.

Time Limit: Time is always important!

Offer Revoked Prior to Acceptance: Between the time when a contract is offered and officially accepted, which may be two or three days, the offeror/buyer can rescind his offer for any reason.

Counteroffer: Negotiating happens a lot in real estate, and the seller will often give a counteroffer. This new counteroffer throws out any previous offers. Nobody is obligated to accept the terms of this new counteroffer.

VALID, VOID, AND VOIDABLE CONTRACTS

A *valid contract*: all legal requirements have been met. (Most contracts are valid — don't worry!)

A *void contract:* something comes up to make the contract not legal. For instance, Mr. Jones may try to sell a property, but if Mr. Jones is not the legal owner of this property, the sale can't go through.

A *voidable contract.* One party can fully void the contract if he or she wishes.

PURCHASE AND SALE AGREEMENTS

Probably the most important document you will encounter is the Purchase and Sale Agreement. Please review the following terms and the sample P&S Agreement shown below. Note that our sample is from the State of New Hampshire, and your specific P&S form will vary slightly. However, all regions have the same basic information needed on their Purchase and Sale forms.

Name of the Parties: Full legal names plus the full address.

Description of the Land: The book and page number (including the date) that the deed is registered in the county registry.

Price (Consideration): Money, or anything else that will be exchanged between the seller and the buyer.

Deposit: Also called *earnest money*. The buyer pays a deposit as part of the down payment on the property, showing that he or she is serious about the purchase. All deposits *must* be held in an escrow account, whether it's the real estate attorney's or the broker's account.

Date: There are two key dates; the date that the contract is signed by BOTH parties and the date of closing.

Signatures: Everyone named in the contract must sign the agreement.

Other terms you need to know

Purchase and Sale Agreement (P&S): This is the form used in a property sale.

Bill of Sale: This form is used for the sale of personal property.

Agreement in Writing: Everything needs to be in writing to be legal.

Breach of Contract: If either person doesn't follow the contract, there is a breach of contract. There can be a court case, for losses that happened because of the breach.

Assignment: An assignment of a contract means to transfer the rights of one party to some other third party.

Novation: An agreement can be formed with a third party to fully replace the first contract.

Caveat Emptor: This means "buyer beware" or "let the buyer beware" and is often a part of most contracts.

DEEDS

A *deed* is a written instrument that transfers ownership of real property from one party to another.

Deeds are recorded in County Land Records or in a Registry of Deeds, in large books logged and stored at the Registry. Their specific numbered registry info is called the property's *deed reference*. The *grantee* of the deed means the buyer, and the *grantor* is the person selling the property.

Every time a property is sold or transferred from one owner to another, a new deed must be created and recorded. When a property owner refinances his or her own home, a new deed is created as well.

Types of deeds

General warranty deed (or a "warranty deed"): This gives the most protection for a buyer, compared to other types of deeds.

Special warranty deed: This guarantees the grantee against any defects or claims that came up during the grantor's period of ownership, but not from before they owned it.

Quitclaim deed: A quitclaim deed gives whatever interest the grantor has in the property but makes no warranties or guarantees as to what they include. Lenders ask for title insurance protection for them, and it is usually a good idea for a buyer to get a "buyer's title insurance policy." You might want this to protect the new buyer against claims brought against them due to potential title issues (such as multiple ownership).

Other types of deeds: Here are some other types of deeds that aren't very common. Talk with your broker or a real estate attorney if you come across any of the following:

- Deed in Trust
- Trustee's Deed
- Bargain and Sale Deed
- Judicial Deed
- Executor's Deed
- Tax Deed
- Sheriff's Deed
- Administration Deed
- Guardian's Deed
- Gift Deed
- Commissioner's Deed
- Referee's Deed in Foreclosure

Main parts of a deed

The main parts of a deed are:

1. Grantor (seller)

2. Grantee (buyer)

3. Consideration (usually money; always something of value)

4. Granting Clause (means the grantor is giving all rights to the grantee)

5. Habendum Clause (means "to have and to hold" and reaffirms the granting clause)

6. Limitations/Deed Restrictions

7. Legal Description (this will include a *metes and bounds*, *lot and block*, and/or a *government survey* method of description; see below)

8. Signature of grantors

9. Delivery and acceptance (to buyer/grantee)

10. Acknowledgement (neither side is under duress)

11. Recording (at the County Registry of Deeds; usually requires a minor fee)

Metes and bounds: Describes the land by the perimeter of a lot, plus the location of the lot line either by compass point (for example, NW 34'8") or by a monument (like an iron pipe, nail, oak tree, or stone wall).

Lot and Block: This refers to a map or "plat" that has been placed on file with the county by a developer. The plat identifies each parcel or lot within a block and assigns numbers to them.

Government Survey: This means the boundaries of towns, townships, and section of towns, and is used by states and local governments, but not really for private pieces of land.

Other important deed and title terms

Torrens System: When land titles are recorded instead of deeds. This system is used in some states for settling land disputes.

Title Search/Title Insurance: The mortgage bank will hire an attorney to perform a title search before the loan is administered. This is to make sure nobody else can claim he or she owns the property. The attorney will then create an *abstract of title* with the information that was found.

Because sometimes mistakes happen in title searches, and the fact that many parcels have been transferred upward of 10 to 20 times officially, most banks and many private buyers will get a specialized insurance policy called title insurance. As with any insurance policy, the issuer will attach a *certificate of liability insurance*, which explains the policy.

Tax Stamps/Excise Stamps: Many states require fees to be paid to the state when a property is transferred from one owner to another. These stamps indicate that the required excise tax has been paid and can be physically affixed to the deed. This is taken care of by the attorney who will add them to the deed that he records with the registry.

Involuntary Alienation: There are several reasons why property can be sold without the owner's consent:

1. **Adverse Possession** (similar to prescription): You can legally own someone else's property after long periods of using and maintaining it under some conditions. If someone uses another's land for more than the time period noted by the state on adverse possession, that person might get something called an *easement of prescription*, allowing the user to continue ownership rights to the property. An *appurtenant easement* gives the right to use adjoining property that transfers with the land, and an *easement in gross* attaches a particular right to a person rather than to the property itself.

2. **Eminent Domain** (also called condemnation): When the government (local, county, state, or federal) takes ownership of the (private) property for specific use of "the common good." Here, the

consent of the property owner is *not* required. However, the government must pay a fair market value for the property.

3. **Escheat**: This is when the state can take title of a property where the owner has died and has no will and no heirs.

4. **Foreclosure**: This is when the bank forces the sale of a property in order to repay a defaulted and delinquent debt.

5. **Natural Forces**: Natural disasters happen. Property, or parts of it, can be lost through them. This is common in seacoast areas and can also happen through tornados, storms, and earthquakes.

Terms to remember: Land that is added to land bordering rivers, lakes, and the sea is called *accretion*. When land is gradually lost over time, that is called *erosion*. A sudden loss of land via a storm or earthquake is called *avulsion*.

Transfer by Will: After a property is transferred because of a will, we say the property is *devised*. The probate court is the legal body that approves and takes care of the legal title transfer.

LEASES AND PROPERTY MANAGEMENT

Many residential or business properties you will work with will not be bought and sold, but will be rented. Sometimes a property management company is involved when a lease happens. Here are several kinds of leases, and some property management basics.

Freehold and non-freehold estates

Freehold means an agreement lasts for an indefinite period of time (more than a lifetime). If an owner has a *fee simple property*, without any limits or conditions, this is a type of freehold estate. In this section, we will instead be discussing non-freehold estate, which is more common.

Non-freehold estates are also called "leasehold" estates. The property owner has most of his or her rights, but gives a portion of them — through a *Right of Possession* — to the tenant. This is in return for some payment to the owner — in the form of *rent* — that follows the details of a *lease*. Leases last only a particular period of time, called the *term*.

Lessor = property owner

Lessee = the tenant (the one paying rent)

Types of leasehold estates (or "tenancies")

Estate at sufferance: When a tenant stays past the lease term or hasn't left after he has been asked to vacate.

Estate at will (also known as tenant/tenancy at will): This is when either side can end the lease agreement at any time, as long as they give proper notice (as written in the contract), with no time limits.

Estate for years: The most common type, where there is a specific amount of time an end date.

Estate from period to period: There are terms, normally month to month or year to year, but no end date. If neither party wants to end the lease when the lease runs out, then the lease continues following the same rules.

Types of leases

Triple net lease (NNN): The tenant pays all the property expenses (utilities, insurance, and taxes) in addition to rent.

Gross lease (straight, flat lease): The owner pays for all expenses (utilities), and the tenant only rent.

Percentage lease: For business owners; when a tenant's business increases, his or her rent will increase.

Graduated (or Step-Up) lease: The rent increases over the course of time. This is used when a company needs lower rent in the beginning of the lease to get a business started.

Ground lease: The leaseholder makes some improvements to the property (like construction, renovations, etc.), and at the end of the lease, the improved property belongs again fully to the legal owner. This usually would mean having a long-term lease, as renters would be unwilling to build costly improvements if they only get to enjoy the updates for a couple of years.

Index lease: The rent chances based on a published record of cost changes.

Sandwich lease: This is a lease that allows subletting (someone else can pay to live on the property besides the original renter).

Sale and leaseback: The seller rents back the property from the buyer.

Lease purchase: Two people will have a lease agreement for a period of time, and then the renter will buy the property.

What do lessors and lessees have to do?

A lease is a contract — both sides have keep up their parts of the bargain. Beyond the details written within the lease, there are some other "common sense" rules that both parties must follow, or face fines and lawsuits.

If a tenant doesn't pay or has too many late payments, he or she can be *evicted* by the owner. There is a legal process to this that the owner must follow.

Usually, renters have to pay a security deposit. This is given in case damage is caused to the property. If damage happens during a lease, the landlord has the right to use some or all of this security deposit to fix the physical damage.

> If someone is using collateral to help get a loan, a *letter of hypothecation* is written where the debtor pledges to give the collateral in case the debt isn't paid, or a third party pledges collateral for the debtor.

Lease options

Sometimes there is an option for the renter to purchase the property from the owner at the end of the lease. Sometimes a part of the rent will then be taken off of the purchase price or the deposit at the time of purchase.

Ehe lessee may have the "right of first refusal" on the property, meaning the seller will give him or her the first chance to buy the property (and end the lease) if the owner has another written offer to purchase the property.

Assignment vs. sublease

If a lessee signs a lease to a third party, then that third party is responsible for all terms in the original agreement.

A lessee may be able to sublease the property to a third party, and still have all the rights and responsibilities of the lease. The renter still has to pay rent and is responsible for the condition of the property. In a sublease, the lessee is letting a third party live on the property, and that third party will pay the rent. Keep in mind that some leases are drafted so the renter *can't* sublease the property.

Other lease terms and considerations

Leases within Property Purchases: If the seller of a property is in the middle of a five-year lease agreement with a tenant, the new owner has to allow the tenant to stay under the same rent and conditions.

99-Year Leases: This is usually the longest lease term allowed by law without being a "permanent" type of agreement.

State Differences and Consumer Protection Laws: For an overview of landlord-tenant laws by state, or landlord legal responsibilities by state, go to: **www.nolo.com/legal-encyclopedia/state-landlord-tenant-laws**.

Property management basics

Your real estate company may have its own property management division. Real estate and property management go hand-in-hand. Property managers take care of:

- Evictions

- Keeping track of accounts for monthly and year-end reports

- Pay the expenses on the property

- Advertise for, screen, interview, and choose tenants

- Collect rents

- Repairs

Property management firms will be the main contact person for the tenants. A property management company also gets an administrative fee. The fee is normally paid every month by the property owner.

As a real estate professional, you will probably be asked to recommend a quality property manager. You can also find out what others are saying about property management firms through Zillow's Property Management Finder, available at: **www.zillow.com/agent-finder/property-manager-reviews**. Here you can see ratings and reviews, so you can research and provide this feedback to your client.

REAL ESTATE BROKERAGE

As a new real estate sales agent, you will be required to work as a "broker" or *on behalf* of a "broker": a person who sells, buys, exchanges, rents, and negotiates real property for others. Brokers can work in different areas of real estate, like buyer or seller representations, rentals and leasing, residential, commercial, retail, industrial, and so forth. The term "broker" may mean more than one person — it could be a partnership, an LLC, or a larger corporation. In this book, when we say "broker," we mean all of those.

Broker-related terms and types of agencies

Principal: This is another name for the broker who hires the sales agent.

Fiduciary relationship: The agent always looks out for the best interest of the broker in all dealings with the clients.

Buyer agency: This is when an agent is representing the buyer, not the seller. The specific agreement will tell whether the commission is paid by the buyer, the listing agent out of the seller's commission, or by the seller in a separate agreement.

Single agency: This is most common — the broker represents either the buyer or seller.

Dual agency: It is possible for one broker to represent both the buyer and the seller in the same property transfer and sale.

Subagents: This is what happens when a listing broker "co-brokers" with another broker to sell the property on behalf of the seller.

Open Listing: When a listing has been given to more than one broker. Any broker can sell the property, and the seller can also sell the property themselves without the use of any broker.

Exclusive Listing: When only one broker is given the opportunity to sell/list the property (this is generally the most common arrangement).

Net Listing: This is when the seller states what he or she wishes to receive, and then any amount over that is given to the broker.

Multiple Listing: A sharing of the listing for practical purposes. (More below.)

Commissions: This is how you and the broker will be paid in a transaction. Normally, the full commission in a residential setting is between four percent and seven percent of the sale price, and often, that is broken down between a listing broker and a co-broker.

Capital gains: These IRS and accounting-based laws are constantly changing, and it is best to follow up with your broker and/or a Certified Public Accountant (CPA) in your area to determine what capital gain ramifications may be of note to your potential seller clients.

REALTOR®: This copyrighted and registered word is reserved only for those members of the NAR who have agreed to their specific Code of Ethics.

Encumbrances: Anything that lessens the value of a property.

Escrow accounts: Agents will often have to make deposits into escrow accounts, which are often held by either their broker or a real estate attorney. An escrow account normally houses a buyer's deposit and may also hold other money.

Termination of Agency: Can happen by any of the following:

1. When the property is sold

2. Time limit expires (most listing agreements are three, six, nine, or 12 months)

3. Both sides mutually agree to stop the arrangement

4. Revocation of either party (this may result in legal action)

5. If either party dies

6. If there is severe damage to the property

7. If either party goes bankrupt

Agent's professional responsibilities and strategies

As a real estate sales agent, it is important to remember and focus on the following professional duties.

Reasonable care and diligence: Always represent your broker with a reasonable degree of skill, care, and diligence.

Accountability: An agent must account for all funds given to his or her control; don't co-mingle any funds (deposits, rents) with his or her own personal money.

Confidentiality: The agent keeps information confidential to both the client and the broker.

Disclosure (also known as Duty of Notice): The agent must disclose any conflicts of interest to their broker (for example, if the agent is related to the property buyer).

Loyalty: The agent must act in the best interest of the broker.

Obedience: The agent must follow all instructions and orders given by the broker, even if those instructions aren't in the agent's best interest.

Here are four keys — the four Ds — of agency strategy:

1. **Document**: Document all important papers, agreements, disclosures, and so on.

2. **Do**: Do follow the rules required by your specific agency contract, state agency law, and fiduciary duties.

3. **Disclose**: Disclose to your client or pending client what all the agency options and relationships are (buyer agency or dual agency, for example).

4. **Decide**: Decide whether you would like to represent the seller, the buyer, or both.

The Multiple Listing Service (MLS)

Each state has its own specific MLS. Only real estate brokers, agents, and appraisers have full access to the MLS. They pay a fee to a third-party company to view and submit property listings.

Marketing strategies and basics

As a sales agent, you will be competing with hundreds of other agents. People will choose you because of a number of factors, like:

1. Experience level

2. Personality

3. Comfort/how well they know you already

4. Relationships (family and friendly connections)

5. Real estate knowledge base

6. The broker or company you are working for

7. Whether you are working as a full-time or part-time agent

8. What your regular listing commission percentage is

9. What, specifically, the client is getting in marketing and advertising services

10. If their listing is on the MLS, and if your office offers co-brokering

11. How well you promote yourself

12. Your track record of success

13. If you appear honest and trustworthy

14. Your online presence

These are a few of the main areas that you will need to focus on as you build your business.

Marketing with the MLS

These days, you can look through thousands of homes. Most people expect that their listing will be posted in the MLS. They want their listing to be viewed quickly by potential buyers, seller brokers, agents, and clients. Your broker can help post your listing on the MLS and keep it up-to-date. However, these are the main steps:

1. Get a signed listing agreement with the seller.

2. Fill out the forms with your state's MLS.

3. Add pictures.

4. State on the system what co-broker percentage you are offering. Usually this is 50 percent of the total listing commission that was agreed upon with the seller.

5. Make sure the listing is updated.

6. Many MLS systems have a means of gathering marketing data to help you compare other properties, and to see how often your listing is being viewed and visited.

Land development and building construction

Here are a few things to keep in mind about new construction:

You will be working with homebuilders and general contractors. You will probably be representing a builder as the seller of a property that is either being built during your listing agreement or has already been completed in full.

If a builder is building a home on a lot but has no end-buyer in mind, it is called a "spec home" or "speculative home."

Give yourself, and the builder, plenty of time. You may need to extend your listing agreement an extra three months during a new construction project. Most construction takes longer than planned.

Property income analysis

Investment property is any property where the owner is expecting monthly cash flow and/or eventual profits as a result of ownership. The property might be rented out to others. Or, some real estate investors will try to quickly buy and sell property quickly, called "flipping."

In most cases, the owner doesn't live on the property. Most likely, a third-party property management company will handle all the details.

CASE STUDY: BEING LICENSED IN MULTIPLE STATES

Al P.
Real Estate Investor, five years

I have been working as a real estate broker for five years in New Hampshire and four years in Florida. About 50 percent of what I do regularly I learned from the license examination materials. In addition, about 25 percent of my activities I learned from my broker training classes, with the remaining 25 percent being learned via the "school of hard knocks"!

One of the key aspects of real estate is internet marketing and website development and betterment, which was not discussed much at all during the pre-exam courses or the exam itself. It may be wise for a new agent to get some outside assistance with this important aspect of the industry.

There is always some type of continuing education requirement. In both Florida and New Hampshire, there is a required state-approved test where I needed to achieve either a 70 percent or 75 percent to pass and receive the credits.

I studied hard for both New Hampshire and Florida licenses. Florida was the hardest. I took the state test three days after taking the class so that everything was still fresh in my mind. I also replayed audio lessons in my car every day before the state test.

● ● ●

CASE STUDY: TAKING THE EXAM SERIOUSLY

Ron F.
Real Estate Agent, 25 years

After 25 years in the real estate business, I have seen nearly everything. During all this time, I have probably used about 70 to 75 percent of what was learned in the real estate licensing exam. Initially, I felt that much of the material was not useful.

Much of what I do every week correlates directly back to items learned in the pre-exam course and its book. As a student, one should take the study seriously. By doing so and applying oneself, it increases learning for education's sake and not just to pass the exam!

After taking the state-mandated pre-exam 40-hour course, I was fortunate enough to pass the exam on the first try. The hardest section of my exam was the minutia about the prorations that take place on the day of closing. As a REALTOR®, I have never been asked about these numbers by any clients. In New Hampshire, we need to take nine hours of continuing education every two years. Three of those hours need to be "core" courses, with the other six being elective subjects.

CHAPTER 3

REAL ESTATE LAW

IN THIS CHAPTER, WE'LL LOOK AT REAL ESTATE LAW, ALONG WITH some important terms you need to know. It is very important to remember the No. 1 rule for a good real estate agent: *Leave the law to an attorney. You're a real estate agent, not a lawyer.*

REAL ESTATE LAW AND REGULATIONS BY STATE

We're not going to jump into comparing all of these details between the laws of each state here. At a minimum, you should review these real estate contracts and forms for your state:

- Purchase & Sale Agreement (P&S)

- Residential Lease Agreement

- Commercial Lease Agreement

- Listing Agreement(s)

- Property Disclosure Statements and Forms (some states require)

- Offer to Purchase Form (used in some states in conjunction with P&S)

- Agent-Broker Agreement

Sometimes, the person you're working with will try to use a generic, national P&S Agreement. This isn't a good idea, because sometimes the basic and national templates do not follow the specific bylaws a state may have for a sale. Later, in a court of law, it could be found to be invalid.

Also, don't change the details in a contract or accepted P&S. The forms that your broker use have been used by various real estate attorneys in your state and approved by your state Board of REALTORS®. More importantly, it's been approved by your state's Real Estate Commission, the governing body of all real estate practice in your state.

BASICS OF LICENSE LAW

The State's Board (or Commission) oversees all brokers and agents in the state and makes sure they are qualified (and licensed). Here are some typical things about these boards:

- Appointed by the Governor (usually five or seven members)

- Has a chairperson, and all will be citizens of the state, *and* experienced real estate brokers and lawyers

- Members usually serve for three to six years

- Usually meet four times a year, where they review important business

- Can create new bylaws and rules about real estate

- Runs the licensing exams for brokers and sales agents

- Can conduct hearings and investigations and sees that all related laws are followed

- Can suspend any broker or sales agent license if necessary (this can be appealed)

- Can fine brokers and agents if not following its bylaws

- Use majority rules to vote

Licensing requirements

Typically, if you do these things, you have to be a licensed agent (and working under a broker):

1. Markets yourself as someone who sells or leases real estate

2. Sells, exchanges, purchases, rents, leases, transfers, makes offers, and lists properties to sell

3. Helps find people who want to buy (or rent) and property to buy (or rent)

4. Helps settle any contract, even if it doesn't that end in a sale.

Typical laws and statutes

Here are some basic rules you will probably find in your state:

- Agents can't place "blind ads," meaning you have to state the name of the company you work for in your marketing.

- A sales agent must work for a broker, and usually only one broker at a time.

- An.agent can be either an employee of the broker or an independent contractor. (Be sure to ask about this as you compare different companies to work for.)

- Commissions are flexible.

- An agent has to tell the buyer and seller who you're working for

- You have to share any offers immediately with the other party. (Don't procrastinate!)

- Give any deposits paid by a buyer immediately to the broker.

- All brokers must have a business address and hang their state broker license/certificate in an obvious location in the office.

- It is illegal for an agent or broker to tell clients they *shouldn't* use a real estate attorney.

- Keep proof of all listings and rental ads for around two to three years, like the Fair Housing Act says.

- Brokers must maintain records of all checks, money orders, and cash deposits for two to three years.

- Real estate schools must be authorized to confirm the hours an agent spends on professional education and credits.

- Board Qualified Instructors (at these schools) have requirements that are even tougher than those of everyday real estate brokers.

CONTRACTS AND LEGAL DOCUMENTS

The two most important things to give your clients are the P&S Agreement and the Lease Agreement (if it's relevant). And REMEMBER: it's not a "contract" unless it is signed, approved, and dated, by *both* sides, and when both sides are aware that the other has accepted. Until then, it's just a piece of paper

You may have heard buyer and seller signatures on a real estate contract have to be *notarized*. This means the person signing has to sign in front of a state-approved Notary Public, after showing ID. Actually, most states don't require this.

Some other clauses you'll see might be:
- *Automatic renewal clause*: another term can continue after the original agreement expires.

- *Limitation of liability clause*: both parties agree on a maximum amount of damages that will have to be paid if the contract is void for some reason in the future.

> • *Broker protection clause*: the broker will get a commission when someone besides the potential buyer purchases the property after the listing agreement expires.

The only thing you should add to a state-specific and authorized real estate form are when there is space given to add extra details — an addendum. An addendum means "an addition or update for an existing contract between parties."

Here's a quick review of the parts you'll see on a Real Estate Contract or Legal Document:

1. **Attorney review clause**: Putting this into the contract gives the attorney time to review it (usually two weeks) and helps protect both buyers and sellers.

2. **Timing or method of payment**: Just saying the price of a house is *not* enough. If part of the total is paid as earnest money (initial deposits and then payments), those details need to be listed, along with the dates when each payment is to be made and how (bank/certified check, wire transfer, or cash).

3. **Mortgage contingency clause**: Most people buying property need financing, so this is important. Without this, a buyer could be responsible to buy the house even if he or she can't get a mortgage.

4. **Defeasance clause**: This says the borrower will be given the title to the property when all the mortgage terms are met.

5. **Inspections clause**: The buyer gets to have licensed professionals inspect the property and cancel the contract if those inspections uncover "unsatisfactory" conditions. This has to be done in a cer-

tain time frame, and the contract states what kind of situations might lead to the contract being cancelled.

6. **Pre-closing damage/destruction clause**: Check out the *doctrine of equitable conversion (see next section)* for more details, but depending on the state, and especially if this piece isn't added to the contract, the buyer might have to take responsibility if the property has damage before the closing.

7. **Prorations**: This is what happens to property taxes and utilities (water, electricity, and heating) if the seller moves out and buyer owns the property between the time each of these bills comes due (a very frequent occurrence). These should be detailed at the time the contract is made and, if possible, settled at the closing.

8. **Fixtures, personal property, and bill of sale**: Everyone remembers to put the house down on the contract, but what about all of those "things" inside the house? Which ones are moving out with the seller? Does the buyer know this? What stays with the house? If this isn't put in writing, it could cause trouble later. A smart real estate agent will help prevent this from happening.

9. **Post-closing possession agreement**: In many cases, the seller will be purchasing a new property and might not be able to move out of the old one by closing day. If this is the case, assuming the buyer agrees to such an extended stay, a final deadline date by which the seller will move out should be included in the real estate contract. If the former owners need to pay rent to the new buyers, a separate agreement should be added to the contract, usually as an addendum. This is a practical issue that comes up again and again.

10. **Condominium/association letters and waivers**: If you're working with a condominium, a house belonging to an association, or is tied together in some other type of group living arrangement or

co-op, certain details should be made clear before signing the P&S Agreement. For example, the buyer needs to talk with the housing association (typically, the buyer's attorney does this) to check if any money is owed to them from this property, to confirm the amount of any current or upcoming fees, and to waive any *right of first refusal* that may be held by the organization.

What happens if the property is destroyed between signing and closing?

In the past, the answer was that the buyer would be responsible. The thinking behind this — called *the Doctrine of Equitable Conversion* — is that although buyer doesn't get the *legal* title to the property when he or she signed the contract, the buyer does get the *title in equity*. In other words, the buyer is called the "true" or *equitable* owner of the property, but the seller's interest is just the right to the money from the sale. Under this rule, the buyer would still have to pay the *full* purchase price to the seller, even if the subject property was destroyed (completely or partially) before closing.

In order to make this more fair, a contract can always have its own rules about losses that happen before closing. A buyer may want something added to the contract that makes the seller responsible for any damage to the property (not caused by the buyer) before the title transfer. Also, the buyer, like the seller, usually can purchase insurance that covers this kind of damage to the property.

FEDERAL FAIR HOUSING LAW

The Federal Fair Housing Law (amended in 1989), came about in 1968 as the Fair Housing Act. We will refer to the Federal Housing Administration with the acronym FHA.

Important parts of the FHA you should know

- No discrimination against "protected classes" (race, color, religion, national origin, sex, handicapped persons, and families with children). "Handicapped" means anybody with physical or mental impairment that limits significant life activities.

- It is illegal for any lender to change the terms of a loan because someone is a member of a protected class — no redlining. "Redlining" is the act of not letting a section of a town get any loans from the bank because of the ethnicity in that area.

- It is illegal to change the terms of, or not offer, brokerage services to members of a protected class.

- It is illegal for an appraiser to lower the price of a property because of its neighborhood. For example, the appraiser can't take off $12,000 on a property because it is located in a minority neighborhood.

- Starting in 1991 for any newly built property with four or more residential units, the following designs have to be handicap-accessible:

1. Lowered light switches and thermostats

2. Hallway and doorway designs

3. Raised electrical outlets

4. Bathrooms and kitchen design

- Does not allow the following activities:

   - Discrimination against any person in setting the terms for a sale or rental

   - Refusal to rent, sell, or otherwise deal with any specific person

   - Discrimination in any advertising

   - Denying that housing is available, when it is

      - *Blockbusting*: trying to convince anybody to sell or rent by telling them that people in a certain class status are entering the neighborhood

      - *Steering*: showing members of a certain ethnicity homes in neighborhoods made up mostly of the same minority background while not showing properties in other neighborhoods that are similar

Housing not covered by the FHA

- Single-family residences

- Rentals of multifamily units that are owner-occupied, as long as it is a two or three family building.

- Religious organizations have a degree of latitude in the sale or rental of properties they own.

- Private clubs (like the Elk Lodge or Kiwanis Club) may sell or rent their property to members only, as long as it is not for commercial purposes.

Enforcement and fines of the FHA

Violations of the FHA are reported through either the Department of Housing and Urban Development (HUD) or the U.S. District Court.

The court may fine the guilty party:

- First offense: $16,000

- Second offense: $42,500 (within five years of first)

- Third offense: $70,000 (within seven years of first)

TRUTH IN LENDING ACT ("REGULATION Z")

Most people need a loan (a mortgage) in order to purchase a property. The Truth in Lending Act (TILA), Title I of the Consumer Credit Protection Act, was created to make sure consumers are informed by making sure they know about all important terms and costs.

TILA is meant to easily help you compare the cost of paying cash versus what you pay in the lifetime of a loan and the difference in this "cost of credit" among different lenders. It also imposes limits on home equity plans (Home Equity Lines of Credit: "HELOC" or Home Equity loans) that are subject to the requirements of certain sections of the act and states the maximum interest that can be charged during a mortgage loan.

Early and final Regulation Z disclosure requirements

TILA says lenders have to make specific disclosures on loans within three business days after their get an application. This first disclosure is mostly based on the unverified information the consumer gave. A final (and more accurate) disclosure statement is given at the closing. The disclosure is in a specific format and includes the following:

1. Name and address of bank or lender

2. Amount financed

3. Breakdown of amount financed

4. Finance charge

5. Annual percentage rate, otherwise known as APR (for definition, see Mortgage Terminology in Chapter 4); this is usually a different number than the mortgage or interest rate

6. Variable rate information (for example, Adjustable-Rate Mortgages [ARM])

7. Payment schedule

8. Total of payments (including all principal plus all interest payments)

9. Demand feature

10. Total sales price

11. Prepayment policy

12. Late payment policy

13. Security interest

14. Insurance requirements

15. Certain security interest charges

16. Contract reference

17. Assumption policy

18. Required deposit information

Disclosure requirements for ARM loans

If the APR on a loan might increase after closing and the term of the loan exceeds one year, other ARM disclosures have to be provided, like:

- The booklet *Consumer Handbook on Adjustable Rate Mortgages*, published by the Consumer Financial Protection Bureau (or something similar). You can find this book by using their search tool at www.consumerfinance.gov.

- A disclosure for every variable-rate program the consumer is interested in. The loan program disclosure gives the important information stated by Regulation Z.

Right of rescission

If the property will be the buyer's main dwelling, there is an option to rescind (get out of) the sale. Lenders should deliver two copies of the notice of the right to rescind and one copy of the disclosure statement to each consumer who is entitled to rescind.

There are specific rules telling how a consumer can legally get out of a credit transaction.

When a consumer rescinds a transaction, it is void, and the consumer is not responsible for any amount, including any finance or interest charge. Within 20 calendar days, the lender has to return any money or property that was given to anyone connected to the transaction, and they have to do whatever is needed to show that the security interest has been terminated.

This can be modified or waived under certain circumstances.

Advertising disclosure requirements

If a lender advertises directly to a consumer, TILA requires the ad to share the credit terms and rate in a certain way. If there is a set rate of finance charge or interest, it may state the rate as an APR. If the rate may be increased after the loan begins (as in many ARMs), the ad must say that. The marketing can't advertise any other rate.

PROPERTY DISCLOSURES AND TRANSFERRING OWNERSHIP

Some states require a seller to fill out and sign a statement about the condition of the property, while other states have no rules about this. All states now recommend you include this kind of good-faith document from the seller and the seller's agent to the potential buyer.

It is the seller's duty (in certain states) to fill out the property disclosure form to the "best of his or her ability." If the seller is really unsure about a property condition, he or she may simply write "unknown." A buyer who notices many "unknowns" on this form should make sure to check out the property, using one or more professional inspectors.

Legally, the seller must state all known property features. There have been lawsuits from situations where the previous owner (seller) is found after the closing to have purposely lied about information on these forms. As an agent, make sure your seller clients understand what their duties are under these laws.

CHAPTER 4
MORTGAGES

BUYING A HOUSE OR PROPERTY PRETTY MUCH MEANS A LOAN with a bank. Most of us don't have a ton of cash just lying around to pay the whole cost of a piece of real estate. In February of 2017, the average price of a single-family home in the United States, for instance, was about $228,400. Without the right amount of money, the buyer will need a loan.

What is "seller financing"? This is where the previous owner will act as a bank and let the buyer pay for the house in payments, using numbers that both the buyer and seller agree on.

A mortgage is a loan that for property like a house, land, or an apartment building. It's also a kind of promissory note (any contract where someone promises to pay someone else back) with certain rules and a certain length of time.

When you're paying a mortgage, you pay a bit of the principal (actual sale cost) plus interest for so many months or years. The total amount you pay by the end of the loan will be higher than the amount you borrowed. Most mortgages are written for a 30-year loan term.

In your day-to-day work as a sales agent you need to know how to figure out monthly payments and escrows based on the mortgage rate, sale price, and other factors.

TAXES

All properties will have to pay some tax, even if it is a very small annual amount. Many banks want to oversee the paying of property taxes to make sure that they are paid. To do this, the bank charges the buyer every month, putting the money in the bank's escrow account. Then, when those taxes are due to the town or county, the bank or the bank's servicing company will pay the bill.

This helps so that once or twice a year the borrower isn't getting a bill in the mail for $6,000. Most Americans would have trouble paying this large amount all at once, but it's easier when it's spread out over the entire year.

REAL ESTATE SETTLEMENT AND PROCEDURES ACT (RESPA)

In 1974, the RESPA was created so we have a specific way to share information about fees and loan terms for residential real estate. It also tries to get rid of unethical practices between real estate agents and banking officers, like kickbacks or referral fees.

RESPA is administered by the Consumer Financial Protection Bureau and is part of every loan backed by the government, like VA and FHA. It also is required of any loans sold to Fannie Mae, Ginnie Mae, and Freddie Mac. Your broker will probably have rules in place to make sure that you don't do anything against RESPA policy.

One-to-four person family homes (as long as the owner also occupies the building) are covered by RESPA, as well as second mortgages (home equity loans). The three key areas you need to know are: Controlled Business Arrangements, Computerized Loan Originations, and the HUD-1 Settlement Statement.

Controlled Business Arrangement (CBA)

CBA is a big part of RESPA. The agency you work for will have its own forms that your clients (buyer and sellers) read and sign. It *is* legal for the real estate agent to mention and discuss loans, but there are forms that you must have that are meant to protect the consumer from being "bullied" into getting a mortgage through your affiliated lender.

In addition, it is very important that you *don't* accept any "referral fees" or anything of value from a mortgage broker or loan officer, even if you are giving business to them. If you get any form of payment, it should be for an actual service you did, not merely referring your client to someone.

Computerized Loan Origination (CLO)

Many real estate agents have their own website with their own online mortgage loan application. Here the potential buyer gives some of their financial information as well as their price range. The real estate agent might submit this information to a lender to get a lender's preapproval for the borrower. You can do this under certain rules if you disclose to the borrower that the agent has these types of business relationships.

HUD-1 — RESPA Uniform Settlement Statement

You should be very familiar with this type of HUD-1 form and its terminology and payouts, and you should be able to explain it in full to your client, be it the buyer or seller.

The HUD-1 settlement statement is a standardized form used at closing that lists all financial information affecting both buyers and sellers. This includes all charges and fees, and all prorations.

A. Settlement Statement

U.S. Department of Housing and Urban Development

OMB Approval No. 2502-0265

B. Type of Loan

| 1. ☐ FHA | 2. ☐ FmHA | 3. ☐ Conv. Unins. | 6. File Number: | 7. Loan Number: | 8. Mortgage Insurance Case Number: |
| 4. ☐ VA | 5. ☐ Conv. Ins. | | | | |

C. Note: This form is furnished to give you a statement of actual settlement costs. Amounts paid to and by the settlement agent are shown. Items marked "(p.o.c.)" were paid outside the closing; they are shown here for informational purposes and are not included in the totals.

D. Name & Address of Borrower:	E. Name & Address of Seller:	F. Name & Address of Lender:

G. Property Location:	H. Settlement Agent:	
	Place of Settlement:	I. Settlement Date:

J. Summary of Borrower's Transaction		K. Summary of Seller's Transaction	
100. Gross Amount Due From Borrower		**400. Gross Amount Due To Seller**	
101. Contract sales price		401. Contract sales price	
102. Personal property		402. Personal property	
103. Settlement charges to borrower (line 1400)		403.	
104.		404.	
105.		405.	
Adjustments for items paid by seller in advance		Adjustments for items paid by seller in advance	
106. City/town taxes to		406. City/town taxes to	
107. County taxes to		407. County taxes to	
108. Assessments to		408. Assessments to	
109.		409.	
110.		410.	
111.		411.	
112.		412.	
120. Gross Amount Due From Borrower		**420. Gross Amount Due To Seller**	
200. Amounts Paid By Or In Behalf Of Borrower		**500. Reductions In Amount Due To Seller**	
201. Deposit or earnest money		501. Excess deposit (see instructions)	
202. Principal amount of new loan(s)		502. Settlement charges to seller (line 1400)	
203. Existing loan(s) taken subject to		503. Existing loan(s) taken subject to	
204.		504. Payoff of first mortgage loan	
205.		505. Payoff of second mortgage loan	
206.		506.	
207.		507.	
208.		508.	
209.		509.	
Adjustments for items unpaid by seller		Adjustments for items unpaid by seller	
210. City/town taxes to		510. City/town taxes to	
211. County taxes to		511. County taxes to	
212. Assessments to		512. Assessments to	
213.		513.	
214.		514.	
215.		515.	
216.		516.	
217.		517.	
218.		518.	
219.		519.	
220. Total Paid By/For Borrower		**520. Total Reduction Amount Due Seller**	
300. Cash At Settlement From/To Borrower		**600. Cash At Settlement To/From Seller**	
301. Gross Amount due from borrower (line 120)		601. Gross amount due to seller (line 420)	
302. Less amounts paid by/for borrower (line 220)	( )	602. Less reductions in amt. due seller (line 520)	( )
303. Cash ☐ From ☐ To Borrower		**603. Cash** ☐ To ☐ From Seller	

Section 5 of the Real Estate Settlement Procedures Act (RESPA) requires the following: • HUD must develop a Special Information Booklet to help persons borrowing money to finance the purchase of residential real estate to better understand the nature and costs of real estate settlement services; • Each lender must provide the booklet to all applicants from whom it receives or for whom it prepares a written application to borrow money to finance the purchase of residential real estate; • Lenders must prepare and distribute with the Booklet a Good Faith Estimate of the settlement costs that the borrower is likely to incur in connection with the settlement. These disclosures are mandatory.

Section 4(a) of RESPA mandates that HUD develop and prescribe this standard form to be used at the time of loan settlement to provide full disclosure of all charges imposed upon the borrower and seller. These are third party disclosures that are designed to provide the borrower with pertinent information during the settlement process in order to be a better shopper.

The Public Reporting Burden for this collection of information is estimated to average one hour per response, including the time for reviewing instructions, searching existing data sources, gathering and maintaining the data needed, and completing and reviewing the collection of information.

This agency may not collect this information, and you are not required to complete this form, unless it displays a currently valid OMB control number. The information requested does not lend itself to confidentiality.

Previous editions are obsolete

form **HUD-1** (3/96)
ref Handbook 4305.2

L. Settlement Charges

			Paid From Borrowers Funds at Settlement	Paid From Seller's Funds at Settlement
700. Total Sales/Broker's Commission based on price $ @ % =				
Division of Commission (line 700) as follows:				
701. $	to			
702. $	to			
703. Commission paid at Settlement				
704.				
800. Items Payable In Connection With Loan				
801. Loan Origination Fee	%			
802. Loan Discount	%			
803. Appraisal Fee	to			
804. Credit Report	to			
805. Lender's Inspection Fee				
806. Mortgage Insurance Application Fee to				
807. Assumption Fee				
808.				
809.				
810.				
811.				
900. Items Required By Lender To Be Paid In Advance				
901. Interest from to @$	/day			
902. Mortgage Insurance Premium for	months to			
903. Hazard Insurance Premium for	years to			
904.	years to			
905.				
1000. Reserves Deposited With Lender				
1001. Hazard Insurance	months @ $	per month		
1002. Mortgage Insurance	months @ $	per month		
1003. City property taxes	months @ $	per month		
1004. County property taxes	months @ $	per month		
1005. Annual assessments	months @ $	per month		
1006.	months @ $	per month		
1007.	months @ $	per month		
1008.	months @ $	per month		
1100. Title Charges				
1101. Settlement or closing fee	to			
1102. Abstract or title search	to			
1103. Title examination	to			
1104. Title insurance binder	to			
1105. Document preparation	to			
1106. Notary fees	to			
1107. Attorney's fees	to			
(includes above items numbers:		)		
1108. Title insurance	to			
(includes above items numbers:		)		
1109. Lender's coverage	$			
1110. Owner's coverage	$			
1111.				
1112.				
1113.				
1200. Government Recording and Transfer Charges				
1201. Recording fees: Deed $; Mortgage $; Releases $				
1202. City/county tax/stamps: Deed $; Mortgage $				
1203. State tax/stamps: Deed $; Mortgage $				
1204.				
1205.				
1300. Additional Settlement Charges				
1301. Survey to				
1302. Pest inspection to				
1303.				
1304.				
1305.				
1400. Total Settlement Charges (enter on lines 103, Section J and 502, Section K)				

SPECIAL AGREEMENTS

You'll soon learn that real estate agents don't just sell homes!

Condos

Condos can be harder to finance because the bank might have more rules than for the sale of a house. Most banks say that a new condo development needs to be at least 50 percent sold out before they will offer a mortgage to a buyer.

Condotels

This is a new idea, a combination of a condo and hotel room. Very few lenders will give a mortgage to a buyer on this type of new development scheme. It's difficult to find loans for condotels because they can't be financed by Freddie Mac or Fannie Mae.

Half-shares or quarter-shares

This is also a new program. It lets two to four different property owners each have their own share of a loan for one property.

REITS (Real Estate Investment Trusts)

This is more of a process involving the purchase of one or more properties where the owners don't live on-site. Most real estate agents don't work much with REITs.

Credit unions

A credit union is a nonprofit lending institution, which is different than a for-profit bank. They can often give better mortgage rates and deals than a regular bank.

State-specific housing authorities and home financing authorities

Most states have specific groups that help low-to-moderate income buyers qualify for a mortgage.

Mobile homes

It can be difficult to get a loan for single and double-wide mobile homes. If a housing unit has a HUD number or stamp on it or on its deed, it is considered "manufactured," and most lenders will not accept this as collateral on a mortgage loan. However, there are other loan options. Most have 20-year terms, and their interest rates are higher than regular mortgages.

Private lending

Besides banks and credit unions, there are also private people, or small groups of private people, who will lend out money for loans. Private money is used when the buyer or the property won't fit into typical lender rules. Many investors use private money. With private loans, rates and points (lender fees) are much higher than regular loans.

Bridge (blanket) loan

What if you need to buy a home but your old home isn't sold yet? Some buyers need to take out a bridge loan. These are usually three to six months in length and help the buyer afford both mortgage payments.

Land contracts

With land contracts, the buyer takes possession while making payments, but the seller holds the title until the payment is made in full.

CASE STUDY: DEALING WITH REFERRAL PARTNERS

David K.
Mortgage Broker, five years

I have been in the mortgage industry for more than five years, and I work for a mortgage broker as a branch manager.

As a mortgage professional, I need to know certain aspects of RESPA to do my job properly. The part of RESPA that I work with daily is proper disclosures and making sure the information on the disclosures is accurate. We must make sure that we are disclosing to the borrower all the required information per RESPA in a timely manner.

My number one goal with referral partners, including real estate agents, is to treat their customers the same way I would want them to treat mine. They can be assured that I will be upfront with the client and provide them with excellent customer service.

Today, the most difficult part of the job is to keep up with the market and changing guidelines. I have to read and understand the guidelines and make sure that you find out as much information as possible on your borrower.

My advice to new REALTORS® is to:

1. **Educate yourself on financing:** I see so many REALTORS® that waste their time on clients that will never get financing.

2. **Partner with a mortgage lender:** Establish at least three relationships with mortgage lenders. Use them all as a resource and refer your client to all three when you can.

3. **Focus:** Pick a market that you want to sell into, and develop a sales strategy as well as goals on how you will sell into this market. Become the "Real Estate Resource" for your market.

4. **Network:** The successful REALTORS® that are selling homes are the ones that are networked well in their market. Referrals are a great way to do business.

• • •

CASE STUDY: REAL ESTATE & AFFORDABLE HOUSING LAW

Jessica B.
Financial Writer, five years

Statistics say that nearly eight million Americans occupy neighborhoods of poverty where at least 40 percent of the residents are below the poverty line. To bring these families above the poverty line, the government provides different kinds of financial aid — rental, housing, and healthcare assistance.

Creating affordable housing opportunities is a key element of any socially responsible housing policy. The government-backed loans provide housing assistance to low-income and poor-credit borrowers who otherwise do not meet the criteria for traditional lending options offered through private lenders, banks, and mortgage companies. Such loans are available even with low down payments and closing costs that are at comparatively lower interest rates. When the government backs a loan for an otherwise unqualified borrower, lenders are more interested to offer the loan, because even if the borrower defaults, the lender will be paid by the government.

REALTORS® should become knowledgeable about FHA loans. FHA loans have flexible qualifying criteria (low income or poor credit). As such, buyers can easily qualify if they fulfill the basic requirements. Any buyer can easily get prequalified for an FHA loan and then look out for suitable homes. Thus, REALTORS® come to know whether they have a customer who's ready to buy before they show any homes. It gets easier for the REALTOR® to find a suitable home for the buyer because the latter is prequalified and more likely to get a mortgage to finance the purchase.

FHA-insured loans are the most popular government-backed loans, and they have the following features:

1. Help in financing 97 percent of the purchase with the remaining 3 percent being the down payment.

2. One can have low credit (580 FICO score) and high debt-to-income ratio (31/43) to qualify for FHA loan.

3. Allow for down payment in the form of assistance programs and gifts.

4. The borrower pays 3.5 percent of the loan amount as upfront mortgage insurance premium at closing. Often the premiums are included into the loan amount. New borrowers with a FICO score of less than 580 are required to put down at least ten percent.

5. FHA 203k loans can help you finance both the purchase and repair work needed for the home.

CHAPTER 5

APPRAISALS (AKA, HOW MUCH IS IT?)

You may have heard the term "appraisal" before. This is a crucial step in any property sale. An appraisal doesn't set the price of a property; it just estimates what the value might be under normal circumstances.

Only a licensed appraiser can appraise a property.

There are different types of appraisal forms used, most of which are accepted by every bank and mortgage company. The different form numbers are set by Fannie Mae and HUD/FHA based on loan program parameters and underwriting guidelines.

Before we talk about how an appraiser arrives at a market value, let's look at what a certified appraisal is and what it isn't.

All of this information points to one big point: *market value*. This is the highest price a buyer is willing to pay and the lowest price a seller is willing to accept.

The market value assumes:

• Both buyer and seller know the property and market in the area

• The property is on the market a reasonable amount of time

• Neither party is being forced to buy or sell ("under duress")

WHEN DO I NEED AN APPRAISAL?

Loans and mortgages

Lending institutions want an appraisal to make sure that their position is secured well enough to lend the money. Most banks lend up to 90 percent of the property's appraised value, and some will lend up to even 97 percent.

Real estate taxes

A town might want an appraisal to be done to help them figure out a property's value.

Insurance

Insurance companies need to make sure they know how much a home is worth in case something happens like a fire or flood or other natural disaster.

Estate settlement

The heirs of an estate might want an appraisal to help them handle inheritance details.

Condemnation

This means the government takes ownership of a property. The government must pay a fair price for the property.

Buying for a business

This happens in a commercial real estate sale, like when a restaurant owner is selling the business *plus* the property.

Exchanges

This has become increasingly popular, thanks to the IRS code 1031. One owner, or investment group, will essentially trade a property for another property. In this type of exchange, everyone needs to figure out a fair market value for both (or all) properties.

WHAT MAKES A PROPERTY GO UP IN VALUE?

The following things can create value in a property.

Transferability: The ability of the owner to sell his or her property without a lot of tough rules to follow.

Demand: How badly someone wants to buy the property.

Utility: You must be able to use the property for its sought-after purpose.

Scarcity: Scarcity of a property is determined by how many comparable properties are available at any particular time in that area.

INFLUENCES AND VARIABLES TO VALUE

Social forces: You will always see population growth, age groups of people in a neighborhood, and size of the families, along with other factors.

Economic forces: The economy can affect job opportunities, industry growth, how easy it is to get mortgages and loans, the cost of living, real estate taxes, and selling prices of other homes.

Physical forces: People have little control over things like the lay of the land, water tables, and whether or not you can access town utilities or drill for a water well.

Governmental forces: City planning, zoning ordinances, and other local bylaws are often very political, and you might not be able to do anything about them.

Highest and best use: Real estate is constantly changing. A property may have a value of $200,000 as a single-family residential lot, but if that neighborhood suddenly becomes zoned commercial, that same (unchanged) property may have a market value of $325,000.

Supply and demand: If there isn't enough of a certain property, its value will go up.

Contribution: Homeowners will often make changes and improvements to the property, and those changes cost money. This doesn't mean the property always goes up in value, but if the value does go up, it is almost always *less* than what was paid for the changes.

Conformity: Properties that have similar properties in their immediate vicinity often hold their values better than something out of the ordinary (such as a three-family house in the middle of a section of town that only has single-family homes).

Plottage (or assemblage): Combining two lots right by each other into a larger lot would then give that lot more use and worth.

Substitution: This theory says that a potential buyer will choose the second or third house they see instead of the first one they saw if it has all the same good points but costs less.

Anticipation: Often, buyers will value a property because they see *anticipated* pleasure in that property or what the house could be with some changes.

Change: Real estate can always change, because of physical or economic reasons.

THE APPRAISAL PROCESS

When a house is being sold, the bank will want to know how much the property is worth. You need an appraisal because the asset (the house or lot) is collateral for the loan. In other words, if the buyer winds up defaulting on the loan, the bank can take the house back so the bank doesn't lose its money.

As an agent, you need to know the steps of an appraisal.

1. Identify the property by street address *and* legal description.

2. Why is the appraisal being done? Who is the client? Is this for a purchase? For a refinance?

3. What type of property is it?

4. Are there any key zoning changes in the neighborhood?

5. Choosing, finding, and analyzing data. The appraisal will need to know construction cost estimates, income statements, and any costs needed to be spent to make the property produce income.

6. Land value estimate: most appraisal forms want a separate value of the land separate from the building on it.

7. Use the three value approaches listed in the next section. It's always best for the appraiser to attempt to use two or three methods, not just one. In most residential appraisals, the market approach is the most important.

8. Reconciliation of value estimates: here is where the appraiser's experience and knowledge will show. No two properties are *exactly* the same, so there must be additions and subtractions calculated to arrive at a fair market value for the subject property. For example, one other home in the neighborhood may have an extra half-bathroom that this property doesn't have. How much value does that add or subtract?

9. Final report: this is the summary in a report that gives the appraiser's final estimated market value of the property.

See Appendix D for a blank sample Uniform Residential Appraisal Report.

Market approach

The market approach, sometimes called the sales comparison approach, is most often used in residential real estate. This is where you compare the property (and its pluses and minuses) to other properties like it in the area. As the key features of the properties are listed, there is a price adjustment right next to it. At the end, there is an "adjusted sale price," which is a fair market value after the comparisons.

Income approach

There are three things to remember when coming up with a value for an income-producing property: market value, net income, and capitalization rate. The basic formula is:

$$Value = Net\ Income\ /\ Capitalization\ Rate$$

Example: A five-family house brings in an income of $700 per apartment per month. The expenses per year are:

Real estate taxes	$3,000
Insurance	$1,500
Utilities	$1,000
Maintenance/Repairs	$1,200
Misc.	$400

The appraiser has looked at similar area investment properties and found that the appropriate cap rate is 12 percent. What should the value of this property be?

Gross (Total) Income = $700 per Unit × 5 units × 12 months = $42,000
Total Expenses = $7,100
Net Income = $42,000 - $7,100 = $34,900
Using the given cap rate of 12 percent, Value = $34,900 / .12 = $290,833

Appraisers also use something called a Gross Rent Multiplier (GRM) to arrive at a quick ballpark value estimate. This is the relationship between a monthly rent and the property's value. For example, a multi-family property sold for $275,000, with a gross (not "net") monthly income of $3,200. The GRM would be 85.9.

$$\$275,000 / \$3,200 = 85.9 \text{ (GRM)}$$

An appraiser might compare this sale with two other multi-family sales in the town to arrive at an average GRM for the area. The appraiser would then use the average GRM to find a quick estimate of value for a multi-family property.

Cost approach

In the cost approach, first you set a value on the land itself and then on building the structures and features using accepted construction costs. Usually, these costs are based on the how much it will cost to build per square-foot.

CASE STUDY: BEING CAUTIOUS ABOUT HOME VALUATIONS

Michael L.
Real Estate Appraiser

I have been working as a real estate appraiser for more than six years. (More recently, I have also been working as a licensed real estate agent as well.) In the past year, the main changes in my business have been a decrease in volume and tightening of lender guidelines.

Many real estate agents (and buyers and sellers) see various home "prices" and "values" in print and online. None of these are certified appraisals. For instance, assessed values can never keep pace with a fluid, changing market. Assessed values are based on historic, not current, market data. Over the past four to five years, instant home valuations are also available on the internet, but they are not very accurate. They have gotten better as technology advances and accurate market data becomes more readily available. In general, I would say "fair market value" changes every six months. "Volatile markets" change plus or minus 10 percent in a 12-month period.

Here's my list of do's and don'ts for listing agents to make friendly with the appraiser during the inspection:

Do arrive on time for the appointment. If the appraiser is having a bad day and has to wait an extra 15 to 20 minutes for you, usually in the rain, it just starts the whole thing off on the wrong foot.

Do bring a copy of the P&S Agreement. A house is only worth what an educated buyer in the market is willing to pay for it, and a signed purchase and sale agreement is the strongest piece of evidence to support your case.

If it is not fully executed yet, give them an unsigned or partial copy and tell them you'll fax or e-mail it to them as soon as a fully signed one is available. They will need the information contained in the P&S for their appraisal report.

Do include a copy of the field card and the deed. You *did* pull both documents when you listed the home, right? The appraiser will most likely have these documents already, but if not, you may have saved them a trip. Plus, it shows a level of professionalism on your part.

Feel free to include relevant comps. With "relevant" being the key word. It is an appraiser's job to research the comps, but if your house is a particularly tricky or unique one, it does not hurt to make some suggestions. If the comps are less than three months old (yes, these days three months is the preferred time frame!), less than a mile away, and within a 25 percent range (smaller or larger) than your house, throw them in the folder.

Appraisers (and the lenders they work for) like to look at *sold* comps. **Do not** tell the appraiser about all the great active listings in the neighborhood that support the purchase price. Active sales do not set the market; closed sales do.

• • •

CASE STUDY: LEARNING BEYOND THE EXAM

Barbara G.
Real Estate Broker, five years

I have been working as a real estate agent for Coldwell Banker Residential Brokerage for about five years. There has been much that I have had to learn after the license exam in order to be successful. I would say I only use about 50 percent of what I learned from the preparation and completion of the exam.

I wish that the exam would focus more on how to write up good written offers. What should be included or excluded? In my opinion, the hardest part of the exam itself was not knowing exactly what section or subject to focus on in my studying. I remember I studied long and hard on one or two subject headings that were rarely touched on in the Massachusetts state exam.

There was no required pre-exam course needed, and as such I did not take any prep course. However, I did pass the exam on my first attempt. In my state, we need 12 hours of continuing education credits every two years, which is not that much compared to some other states.

CHAPTER 6
MATH REVIEW FOR THE REAL ESTATE AGENT

Basic math skills are necessary to do a good job on the real estate exam. We're going to review some math basics, including some examples and problems. There is an answer key to these problems at the end of the chapter.

DECIMALS

A decimal divides a whole number into subdivisions of tens.

$$\tfrac{1}{5} = .20$$

$$\tfrac{1}{5} \text{ of } \tfrac{1}{5} \text{ [or } \tfrac{1}{25}] = .04$$

Addition of decimals

Line up the decimal points and then add the numbers like any other numbers, making sure to put the decimal point at the bottom in the answer. (Remember that the number .2 can also be written as 0.2 or .20)

Example: 1.12 + .4 + 6.3 =   1.12
                                    .40
                                 + 6.30
                                  7.82

Subtraction of decimals

Like adding decimals, make sure you line up the decimal points for the numbers being subtracted, and then subtract like normal.

Example: 2.34 − 1.03 =   2.34
                              − 1.03
                               1.31

Go ahead and try out the following decimal problems:

1) 16.24 – 4.07 =

2) 14.30 + .78 =

3) 2.2 + 1.45 =

4) 3.29 – 1.20 =

5) 5.67 – 4.07 =

6) 0.02 + 0.102 =

Multiplication of decimals

Here we do *not* line up the decimal points. Instead, multiply the numbers like normal and then add the quantity of decimal points in each number to arrive at the number of digits to the right of the decimal point in the answer.

Example: .35 × .03 = .0105 (or 0.0105)

Try the following decimal problems:

7) 1.0 × 5.67 =

8) 0.1 × 56.70 =

9) 212.08 × 2.5 =

10) 0.02 × 100.09 =

11) 1.6 × 6.1 =

12) 4 × .25 =

Division of decimals

The number on the left is called the "divisor" and the number on the right is called the "dividend." (The answer is the "quotient".) For example:

$$4 \longrightarrow \textbf{dividend}$$
$$\textbf{divisor} \longleftarrow 2\overline{)8} \longrightarrow \textbf{quotient}$$

However, here is an easier way of showing division:

$$8 / 2$$

(In this format, 8 is the dividend and 2 is the divisor. 2 is going into 8. The answer is 4.)

When dividing decimal numbers, the decimal has to be "removed" from the divisor, by moving to the right within the number until the decimal point is right after the last (nonzero) number. However, to calculate the math correctly, one must do the same — move the decimal point to the right, to the other number (the dividend) — by the same amount.

$$4.5 / .20 = 22.5 \text{ (or } 22.50)$$

Practice with these decimal problems:

13) 10.4 / 3.25

14) 56 / 0.3

15) 3.34 / 0.12

16) .8 / 4.2

17) .15 / 0.5

18) 35.4 / 1.6

FRACTIONS

Any number that's not a whole number must be shown as a fraction. When we say "one half," we write it like ½.

Here are some fraction terms you need to know:

Numerator: This is the top number of a fraction. For example, the number 1 in the fraction ½ is the numerator.

Denominator: This is the bottom number of a fraction. For example, the number 2 in the fraction ½ is the denominator.

Proper Fraction: This is when a fraction is less than 1. For example, ¼ (or one quarter) is less than 1.

Improper Fraction: This is when a fraction is more than 1. For example, is more than 1.

Mixed number: This is a whole number plus a fraction. For example, 3 ½ is a mixed number.

Addition of fractions

1) To be added, fractions must have the same denominator.

2) If needed, fractions should be converted into their lowest common denominator (LCD).

3) Once you have the same denominator, you can add the numerators — leaving the denominator as the LCD.

4) Mixed numbers need to be changed to improper fractions before adding.

5) Answers are then converted back to mixed numbers (from improper fractions).

6) Reduce, if needed.

Example

Problem: ⅔ + ⅙

The LCD is 6.

Therefore, change the fraction ⅔ to 4/6

Now, add. $\frac{4}{6} + \frac{1}{6} = \frac{5}{6}$

Try the following fraction problems:

19) $\frac{3}{4} + \frac{1}{2} =$

20) $\frac{4}{7} + \frac{10}{14} =$

21) $1\frac{1}{3} + \frac{5}{6} =$

22) $\frac{8}{2} + \frac{2}{3} =$

23) $2\frac{1}{6} + \frac{3}{4} =$

Subtraction of fractions

In subtraction, the basic rules of adding fractions are maintained.

1) To be subtracted, fractions must have the same denominator.

2) If needed, fractions should be changed to their LCD.

3) Numerators are then subtracted, while the denominator should be the same as the LCD.

4) Mixed numbers need to be converted to improper fractions before subtracting.

5) Answers are then changed back to mixed numbers (from improper fractions).

6) Reduce, if needed.

Example

Problem: 1 ¾ − ⅚

Change 1 ¾ to a single fraction: 7/4

The problem now looks like this: 7/4 − ⅚

The LCD is 12.

Now, change the initial problem to the following: $^{21}/_{12} - ^{10}/_{12}$

Now, subtract. $^{21}/_{12} - ^{10}/_{12} = \mathbf{^{11}/_{12}}$

See what you can do with the following fraction problems:

24) ¾ − ½ =

25) 1 ½ − ⅚ =

26) 2 ⅖ − 4/10 =

27) 6/4 − ⅜ =

28) ¾ − 1/12 =

Multiplication of fractions

Multiplication of fractions can be written three ways:

1) ⅓ × ½ =

2) ⅓ * ½ =

3) ⅓ (½) =

Here are the basic rules of multiplying fractions.

1) Change mixed numbers to improper fraction (i.e., change 3 ½ to 7⁄2)

2) In multiplication, you don't need to convert to the lowest common denominator.

3) Multiply the numerators together.

4) Multiply the denominators together.

5) Reduce, if needed.

6) Convert answer from an improper fraction to a mixed number, if needed.

Example

Problem: 2 ⅓ × 2⁄7

Change 2 ⅓ to a single fraction: 7⁄3

The problem now looks like this: 7⁄3 × 2⁄7

7⁄3 × 2⁄7 = (7 × 2) / (3 × 7) = 21⁄14

Reduce 21⁄14 to 3⁄2

The answer is: **1 ½**

Complete the following fraction problems:

29) ⅔ × 4 ¼ =

30) ½ × 6 ⅙ =

31) ½ × ¼ =

32) 10 ⁴⁄₆ × ⁶⁄₄ =

33) 2 ²⁄₇ × ¹⁄₁₀ =

Division of fractions

Hang with us, because this might sound tricky, but it really isn't. The language used with division sounds like this: the divisor into the dividend equals the quotient (the quotient is the answer). In an equation, this will appear like: Dividend/Divisor = Quotient.

Here are the basic rules of dividing fractions.

1) Change mixed numbers to improper fractions.

2) In division, there is no need to convert to the LCD.

3) Invert (flip) the numerator and denominator of the second number in problem.

4) Continue as if you were multiplying (see steps above).

Example

Problem: [⁴⁄₇] / [²⁄₃]

Flip the numerator and denominator of the second number: "²⁄₃" "³⁄₂"

Now, multiply. ⁴⁄₇ × ³⁄₂ = ¹²⁄₁₄

Reduce. The answer is: ⁶⁄₇

Work on these fraction problems:

34) [⅔] / [½] =

35) [2 ⅓] / [¾] =

36) [1 ⅞] / [⅖] =

PERCENTAGES

Percentage is a means of expressing a part of a whole, where the whole is taken to be "100." If we considered a dozen eggs as the whole, or 100 percent, and three of the dozen were broken from the store, we would say that ³⁄₁₂ were broken, or 25 percent.

When working with percentages in real estate, you have to be able to convert the percentage to either a fraction *or* a decimal to then go forward with the calculation.

Let's look at how we make those conversions — and back again.

Percent to decimal

To convert a percent to a decimal, simply drop the percent sign and move the decimal point *two* places to the *left.*

Example

Problem: 35 percent

Drop the percent: 35 percent = 35

Move the decimal two places to the left: **.35** (or **0.35**)

Try these percentage problems:

37) 50 percent =

38) 110 percent =

39) 6 percent =

40) 25.4 percent =

Decimal to percent

To convert a decimal to a percent, move the decimal point *two* places to the *right*, and add the percent sign.

Example

Problem: .15

Move the decimal two places to the right: .15 = 15

Add the percent sign: **15 percent**

Complete the following decimal problems:

41) 2 =

42) 76 =

43) .04 =

44) 13.23 =

Percent to fraction

To change a percent to a fraction, put the number over 100, drop the percent sign, and then reduce the fraction (to the greatest common divisor if applicable).

Example

Problem: 12 percent

Put the number over 100: $^{12}/_{100}$

Reduce the fraction: $^{3}/_{25}$

Work on the following percentage problems:

45) 8 percent =

46) 34 ½ percent =

47) 45 percent =

48) 123 percent =

Fraction to percent

To convert a fraction to a percent, multiply the number by 100 and add the percent sign. If the fraction is a mixed number, first change it to an improper fraction.

Example

Problem: $\frac{3}{12}$

Multiply by 100: $\frac{3}{12} \times \frac{100}{1} = \frac{300}{12}$

Reduce and add the percent sign: **25 percent**

Try to finish the following fraction problems:

49) $\frac{7}{8}$ =

50) $\frac{1}{4}$ =

51) 2 $\frac{3}{4}$ =

52) = $\frac{5}{4}$

Decimal to fraction

To convert a decimal to a fraction, first take away the decimal point and put the number over 1 multiplied by as many zeros as there are decimal places. Reduce the answer if needed.

Example

Problem: .20

Remove decimal point: 20

Put the number over 1 multiplied by as many zeroes as there are decimal places: $^{20}\!/_{100}$

Reduce. The answer is: $^1\!/_5$

Now look at these decimal problems:

53) .32 =

54) .120 =

55) .8 =

56) 18.5 =

Fraction to decimal

To change a fraction to a decimal, divide the denominator into the numerator. If the number is a mixed number, you must first convert it to an improper fraction.

Example

Problem: 2 ⅔

Convert to an improper fraction:

Divide the denominator into the numerator. The answer is: **2.67**

Complete the following fraction problems:

57) ⅓ =

58) 4 ¼ =

59) 2 ⅕ =

60) ³⁄₁₀ =

MEASUREMENT OF DISTANCE, AREA, AND VOLUME

As a realtor, you're going to have to work with measurements. You might see questions like these:

- How many acres of land are part of this development? (Note: 1 acre = 43,560 square feet, which is close to the size of a football field.)
- Are you listing any 1,500 square-feet, cape-style homes?
- How many miles away is the closest fire station?

We will first review the following key points: area, volume, acreage, and perimeter.

Area

We use the term "square" when talking about area, like when we say square feet or square miles. Whenever you multiply area or volume, you can only multiply "like" units of measure. (So, you can't multiply 5 feet by 20 centimeters.)

When you say squared, you're multiplying a number by the same number. For example, "4 squared" is 4 × 4. The answer would be 16.

Rectangle

A rectangle is a four-sided shape where all angles (the corners) are right angles (90 degrees).

The basic equation for a rectangle is Area = Length × Width.

width   Area = *l* • *w*

length

Example

Problem: How many square feet are in a rectangular lot that is 125 feet long × 200 feet wide?

Answer: 125 feet × 200 feet = **25,000 square feet**

Triangle

A triangle is any three-sided figure. A "right triangle" is a triangle that has one angle that is a right angle (90 degrees).

The basic equation for any triangle is Area = ½ (Base × Height)

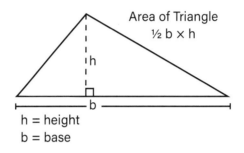

h = height
b = base

Trapezoid

A trapezoid has four sides, and only two sides are parallel. The other two (opposite) sides are not parallel to each other. It's like a "squashed" rectangle or square.

The basic equation for a trapezoid is Area = $\frac{1}{2}$ $(B_1 + B_2)(H)$, where B_1 and B_2 are the lengths of the two sides which ARE parallel to each other, and H is the height or the distance that B_1 and B_2 are apart.

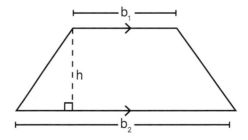

Circle

The area of a circle is pi (π times the radius squared. π = approximately 3.14 or 3 $\frac{1}{7}$.

The radius of a circle is half of the diameter; the diameter is the longest straight line drawn from one side of the circumference to the opposite side of the circle.

DESIGN: INSERT FIGURE EXAMPLE OF A CIRCLE WITH RADIUS (R) & DIAMETER (D) FROM ORIGINAL DESIGN FILES

Example

Problem: What is the area of a circular lot whose radius is 200 feet?

The equation would be π × 200 squared.

Area = 3.14 × (200)(200)

Answer: 3.14 × 40,000 = **125,600 square feet**

Complete the following problems:

61) What is the area of a square lot with street frontage of 225 feet?

62) What is the area of a rectangular lot that is 150 feet wide and 300 feet deep?

63) What is the area of a triangular lot where two sides are 100 feet and 125 feet, if the angle between the two sides is 90 degrees?

64) What is the area of a triangular lot with a base of 300 feet and a height of 150 feet?

65) What is the area of a lot shaped like a trapezoid with these sides: 75 feet, 45 feet, 125 feet, and 45 feet, plus a height of 40 feet (see below)?

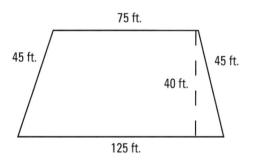

66) What is the area of a circular lot with a diameter of 300 feet?

67) What is the area of a man-made circular pond with a radius of 80 feet?

Acreage

An acre is 43,560 square feet. To easily grasp the size, keep in mind that an acre is about the size of a football field.

Today, you can find sites online to calculate any measurement, but if you do it yourself, the formula for changing square feet to acres is [acres = ft² ÷ 43,560]. Conversely, the formula for changing acres into square feet is [ft² = acres × 43,560].

Volume

In everyday real estate tasks, you'll use area more often than volume, but there will be times when you need to know the volume of something. While area is two-dimensional, volume is three-dimensional.

Remember that **Area** = Length × Width (two measurements being calculated together), whereas **Volume** = Length × Width × Height (three measurements being calculated together).

Rectangular Volume

The volume of a rectangular figure (which would include a square shape) is length × width × height (or depth).

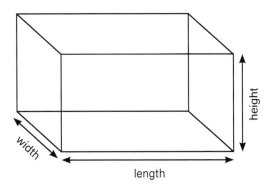

Example

Problem: What is the volume of a room that is 12 feet wide × 18 feet long × 8 feet high?

Use the equation V = L × W × H.

Answer: 12' × 18' × 8' = **1,728 cubic feet (or c.f.)**

Triangular Volume

The volume of triangular shape is ½ the base times the height times the length.

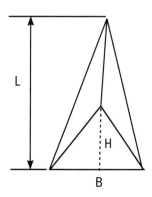

Example

Problem: What is the volume of a camping tent that has a base width of 7 feet, a height of 6 feet, and a length of 10 feet?

Use the equation V = ½ base × height × length.

Answer: ½ (7' × 6') × 10' = **210 cubic feet**

Cylinder (Circular Volume)

The volume of a cylinder is the area of the circular base (3.14 × radius squared) times the height.

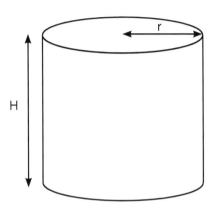

Example

Problem: What is the volume of a cylinder 4 feet high with a base whose diameter is 6 feet?

First, convert the diameter measurement to a radius measurement. R equals ½ the diameter.

R = ½ (6) = 3

Now, use the equation V = (3.14 × radius squared) × height

Answer: 3.14 (3')(3') × 4' = **113.04 cubic feet**

Complete the following problems:

68) An A-Frame type ski chalet is in the shape of a triangle. To determine the size of an air-conditioning unit, the cubic footage of space inside needs to be determined. The roof height is 24 feet, the base width is 24 feet and the base length is 28 feet. What's the volume of this chalet?

69) A cylindrical barrel has a base radius of 1.5 feet and a height of 3.5 feet. What is its volume?

70) What is the volume of a basement whose dimensions are 34 feet long, 24 feet wide, and 7.5 feet high?

Perimeter

Perimeter is the distance around the outside of a shape. For shapes that aren't circles, you just add all the sides together. For circles, the perimeter is called a circumference. The calculation involves π. The perimeter of a circle is (π)(D), where D is the diameter.

Examples

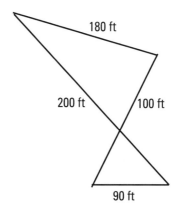

Answer: 100' + 90' + 200' + 180' = **570 feet (or lineal feet)**

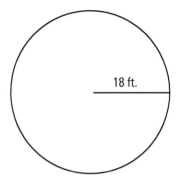

Answer: (3.14)(36') =**113.04 feet**

Complete the following problems:

71) What is the perimeter of a pentagon-shaped lot with dimensional sides of 225 feet, 130 feet, 87 feet, 200 feet, and 32 feet?

72) What is the perimeter of a triangle with a base of 8 feet and both sides measuring 6 feet?

73) What is the perimeter of a circular pool with a diameter of 16 feet?

FORMULAS AND FORMULA AIDS

You will have to know math definitions on the test, but you also need to be able to use a formula to find the correct answer. Most formulas are simple multiplication and division problems, often in fraction form.

Check out the Table of Formula Aids to help you answer the exam's math problems. Feel free to use this guide as you are try the practice exam at the end of this book. Ask your state's testing facilitator if you can bring such a general formula guide into your examination. If you are someone who prefers using an app, iTunes offers a free one called "Real Estate Licensing Exam Prep" that offers flash cards and study guides.

Table of Formula Aids

Formula	Aid
Length x Width = Area L x W = A	$\dfrac{A}{L \times W}$
Principal x Rate x Time = Interest P x R x T = I	$\dfrac{I}{P \times R \times T}$
Base x Rate = Percentage B x R = P	$\dfrac{P}{B \times R}$
*Sell Price x Rate = Commission SP x R = C	$\dfrac{C}{SP \times R}$
*Amount x Rate = Interest A x R = I	$\dfrac{I}{A \times R}$
*Appraised Value x Assessment Rate AppV x AssR = AssV = Assessed Value	$\dfrac{AssV}{AppV \times AssR}$
*Assessed Value x Tax Rate = Annual Tax AssV x TR = Tax	$\dfrac{Tax}{AssV \times TR}$
*Cost x Depreciation Rate = Depreciation C x R = D	$\dfrac{D}{C \times R}$
*Investment x Rate of Profit = Profit I x R = P	$\dfrac{P}{I \times R}$
* Investment x Rate of Loss = Loss I x R = L	$\dfrac{L}{I \times R}$
*Investment x Rate of Return = Net Income I x R = NI	$\dfrac{NI}{I \times R}$
*Value x Capitalization Rate = Net Income V x CR = NI	$\dfrac{NI}{V \times CR}$

OTHER MATH NOTES AND USEFUL TERMS

As a real estate agent, you need to understand important math terms and functions, and we will highlight many of those here. Please refer to the Table of Formulas above, which will correspond to the terms described.

Interest

Interest is the charge for a loan or mortgage.

Interest equals P × R × T.

P = Principal (the amount borrowed)

R = Rate (the percent charged for using the money)

T = Time (the length of the loan)

If the loan is stated in years, and the total length isn't a whole year (for example, two years and three months), use fractions or decimals to make it work in your formula. For example, two years and three months = 2.25 years.

> **Just so you know, bank loans assume there are 30 days in every month, even though many months don't have exactly 30 days in them. It helps keep the math simple.**

Amortization

Amortization is a debt regularly going down, used a lot in mortgages. A 30-year mortgage amortizes (is fully paid off) in exactly 30 years. There are many tables, charts, calculators, and online tools you can use to determine the exact values at different times during a loan term.

In typical mortgages, each month the borrower makes a principal payment as well as an interest payment. Using the example above, after 30 years, the loan's principal amount and all interest payments are completely paid in 30 years. There are "interest-only" mortgages that don't pay down any principal for a period of time. These types of mortgages might not be the best idea, since they don't build equity in the property.

Profit and loss

In real estate, accountants keep track of the numbers to figure out profit and loss (P&L), and what's most important is the return on investment (ROI). For example, if a man invests $8,000 and one year later his investment has grown to $10,000, he has a 25 percent profit, not 20 percent. We must compare the $2,000 profit to the original $8,000 amount.

Investment

Normally, this is equal to the purchase price. This is the amount of money the buyer puts into the investment.

Net income

This is the income minus all expenses every year. For example, if you see an apartment complex for $200,000 and it earns 10 percent every year, there is an annual net income of $20,000.

Rate of return

The rate of return compares the net income to the investment as a percentage.

Taxation

Taxes are paid on different levels — including federal, state, county, and town. Real estate agents work with property taxes, which are normally collected by either the town or the county.

In general, the Assessed Value × Tax Rate = Annual Tax.

The owner pays the annual tax. Normally, the town expects payment either twice or four times per year. When a mortgage is involved, most banks let you (and actually prefer) escrow for the property taxes each month. This way, a smaller portion is paid every month and set aside in the escrow account. Then the escrow account pays the property taxes.

Remember, an appraisal is *not* the same as an assessment. You do an assessment just to determine how much tax to pay.

Tax rates can be said different ways, and different towns or counties may figure them differently, so don't assume. You may see tax rates as so much money per $1,000, per $100, per $10 of assessed value and so on. Some towns use a mill rate (sometimes called a millage rate). A mill rate of 52 = $52/$1,000 of assessment.

Proration and settlement

At closing, there are always charges that need to be calculated between buyer and seller. In most cases, the mortgage lender and the real estate attorney will find the exact dollar figures that each party should pay, based on what day of the month the closing is on. However, it is important for any real estate agent to know how to figure out these values or at least be able to double-check the numbers for their client.

A debit means money coming *from* a party. A credit means money going *to* a party.

Some things that must be prorated and settled at closing are:

1. Property taxes

2. Interest charge on the new and old mortgage loan

3. Utility bills or unused fuel remaining at the home (like propane and oil tanks for home heating)

4. State or county property *transfer* taxes (if applicable in your area)

5. "Stamps" as they are often called — referring to the county registry that stamps the new deed created

As shown below, the physical settlement form is called an HUD-1 Settlement Statement. This is the generic sheet approved by the federal Housing and Urban Development department. On this sheet, you will see the critical figures that a buyer, seller, and agent review before and during the closing.

L. Settlement Charges		Paid from Borrower's Funds at Settlement	Paid from Seller's Funds at Settlement
700. Total Sales / Broker's Commission: $8,186.10			
Division of Commission (line 700) as follows			
701. 4,093.05 to ▮▮▮▮▮▮▮▮▮			
702. 4,093.05 to ▮▮▮▮▮▮▮▮▮▮			
703. Commission Paid at Settlement			8,186.10
704. Warehousing Fee			
800. Items Payable in Connection with Loan:			
801. Our origination charge	(from GFE #1)		
	$1,675.00		
802. Your credit or charge (points) for the specific interest rate chosen	(from GFE #2)		
	$-200.00		
803. Your adjusted origination charges	(from GFE #A)	1,475.00	
804. Appraisal Fee	(from GFE #3)		
to Executive Appraisal Solutions, Inc.		390.00	
805. Credit Report	(from GFE #3)		
to Kroll Factual Data		15.93	
806. Tax Service			
807. Flood Certification	(from GFE #3)		
to First American Flood		13.00	
808. Guarantee Fee	(from GFE #3)		
to USDA		2,857.14	
900. Items Required by Lender to be Paid in Advance:			
901. Daily interest charge from ▮▮▮▮▮▮▮▮▮▮▮▮▮▮▮ days	(from GFE #10)	34.24	
902. Guarantee Fee	(from GFE #3)		
903. Homeowner's Insurance for 1.00 years	(from GFE #11)		
to AIIC		915.00	
1000. Reserves Deposited with Lender:			
1001. Initial deposit for your escrow account	(from GFE #9)		
to Inlanta Mortgage, Inc.		1,563.23	
1002. Homeowner's Insurance 3 months @ $76.25 per month			
to Inlanta Mortgage, Inc.	$228.75		
1003. Mortgage Insurance			
1004. Property Taxes 11 months @ $153.34 per month			
to Inlanta Mortgage, Inc.	$1,686.74		
1005. USDA Annual Fee 2 months @ $47.26 per month	$94.52		
1099. Aggregate Adjustment	$-446.78		
1100. Title Charges:			
1101. Title services and lender's title insurance	(from GFE #4)	800.95	
1102. Settlement or Closing Fee			
to ▮▮▮▮▮▮▮▮▮▮▮▮▮▮	$475.00		697.50
1103. Owner's Title Insurance ▮▮▮▮▮▮▮▮▮▮▮▮▮	(from GFE #5)		
to ▮▮▮▮▮		757.50	
1104. Lender's Title Insurance ▮▮▮▮▮▮▮▮▮			
to ▮▮▮▮▮▮			
- Lender's Premium (Risk Rate Premium: $57.00)	$182.00		
- Endorsement 8.1	$50.00		
- Endorsement FL Form 9	$93.95		
1105. Lender's Title Policy Limit $142,857.00			
1106. Owner's Title Policy Limit $136,435.00			
1107. Agent's Portion of the Total Title Insurance Premium	$758.41		
1108. Underwriter's Portion of the Total Title Insurance Premium	$325.04		
1109. Title Search $85 Paid Outside of Closing FATIC by OLTIA			
1200. Government Recording and Transfer Charges:			
1201. Government Recording Charges	(from GFE #7)	105.00	
1202. Deed $10.00 Mortgage $95.00 Releases $0.00			
1203. Transfer Taxes	(from GFE #8)	785.86	
1204. City/County tax/stamps Deed $0.00 Mortgage $0.00			
1205. State tax/stamps Deed $955.50 Mortgage $500.15			955.50
1206. Intangible Tax			
to Clerk of the Circuit Court	$285.71		
1207. Other Tax 2			
1208. Title Clearing Affidavit (3 Liens)	(from GFE #7)		
to Clerk of the Circuit Court			18.50
1300. Additional Settlement Charges:			
1301. Required services that you can shop for	(from GFE #6)	350.00	
1302. Survey Inspection			
to ▮▮▮▮▮▮▮▮▮▮▮▮▮	$350.00		
1303. Pest Inspection			
1304. 2013 RE Taxes PA# 35996-018-00 Paid Outside of Closing by Seller $1,784.87			
1305.			
1306.			
1400. Total Settlement Charges (Enter on line 103, Section J and line 502, Section K)		$10,062.85	$9,857.60

Comparison of Good Faith Estimate (GFE) and HUD Charges

Charges That Cannot Increase	HUD Line No.	Good Faith Estimate	HUD
Our origination charge	# 801	1,675.00	1,675.00
Your credit or charge (points) for the specific interest rate chosen	# 802	-200.00	-200.00
Your adjusted origination charges	# 803	1,475.00	1,475.00
Transfer taxes	#1203	2,241.36	785.86

Charges That In Total Cannot Increase More Than 10%	HUD Line No.	Good Faith Estimate	HUD
Government Recording Charges	#1201	105.50	105.00
Appraisal Fee	# 804	390.00	390.00
Credit Report	# 805	30.00	15.93
Flood Certification	# 807	13.00	13.00
Guarantee Fee	# 806	2,857.14	2,857.14
Total		3,395.64	3,381.07
Increase between GFE and HUD Charges		-14.57	-0.43%

Charges That Can Change	HUD Line No.	Good Faith Estimate	HUD
Initial deposit for your escrow account	#1001	1,084.58	1,563.23
Daily interest charge from Jul 30, 2014 to Aug 1, 2014 @ 17.1200 / day for 2 days	# 901	462.24	34.24
Homeowner's Insurance	# 903	920.00	915.00
Title services and lender's title insurance	#1101	975.00	800.95
Owner's Title Insurance	#1103	790.00	787.50
Survey Inspection	#1302	350.00	350.00

Loan Terms

Your initial loan amount is	$142,857.00
Your loan term is	30 years
Your initial interest rate is	4.375 %
Your initial monthly amount owed for principal, interest, and any mortgage insurance is	$713.26 includes [X] Principal [X] Interest [ ] Mortgage Insurance
Can your interest rate rise?	[X] No. [ ] Yes, it can rise to a maximum of ____%. The first change will be on _____ and can change again every _____ after _____. Every change date, your interest rate can increase or decrease by ____%. Over the life of the loan, your interest rate is guaranteed to never be LOWER than ____% or HIGHER than ____%.
Even if you make payments on time, can your loan balance rise?	[X] No. [ ] Yes, it can rise to a maximum of $_____
Even if you make payments on time, can your monthly amount owed for principal, interest, and mortgage insurance rise?	[X] No. [ ] Yes, the first increase can be on _____ and the monthly amount owed can rise to $_____ The maximum it can ever rise to is $_____
Does your loan have a prepayment penalty?	[X] No. [ ] Yes, your maximum prepayment penalty is $_____
Does your loan have a balloon payment?	[X] No. [ ] Yes, you have a balloon payment of $_____ due in ____ years on _____
Total monthly amount owed including escrow account payments	[ ] You do not have a monthly escrow payment for items, such as property taxes and homeowner's insurance. You must pay these items directly yourself. [X] You have an additional monthly escrow payment of $276.85 that results in a total initial monthly amount owed of $990.11. This includes principal, interest, any mortgage insurance and any items checked below: [X] Property taxes [X] USDA Annual Fee [ ] Flood Insurance [ ] [X] Homeowner's Insurance [ ]

Note: If you have any questions about the Settlement Charges and Loan Terms listed on this form, please contact your lender.

Buyers

Sellers

Property Addresses

I have carefully reviewed the HUD-1 Settlement Statement, and to the best of my knowledge and belief, it is a true and accurate statement of all receipts and disbursements made on my account or by me in this transaction. I further certify that I have received a copy of HUD-1 Settlement Statement.

Borrower: _____   Seller: _____

The HUD-1 Settlement Statement which I have prepared is a true and accurate account of this transaction. I have caused or will cause the funds to be disbursed in accordance with this statement.

Date: _____

Settlement Agent: _____

WARNING: It is a crime to knowingly make false statements to the United States on this or any other similar form. Penalties upon conviction can include a fine and imprisonment. For details see Title 18 U.S. Code Section 1001 and Section 1010.

Commissions

You'll want to know about commissions as a real estate agent, as it's the way you will get paid most often. Agents share their commissions with their broker, and the broker might sometimes share the total commission with a co-broker.

A seller signs an agreement with an agent to list, market, and sell the property for a percent of the purchase price, which is usually between 4 percent and 6 percent. Here's an example:

- Property sales price (not the *listing price*) = $300,000

- Seller's agreement with listing broker = 5.0 percent = $15,000 **total commission**

- Listing broker splits commission with buyer's broker = $7,500 seller's commission

- Sales agent has negotiated a 60 percent / 40 percent split with his broker.

- 60 percent of $7,500 = **$4,500**

Note that **S**ell **P**rice × **C**ommission **R**ate = **C**ommission (SP × CR = C)

Depreciation

Depreciation means a property's value is going down. This happens for different reasons, but, in general, it is looked at by the IRS and all investors, property managers, and owners. The IRS says that only buildings can depreciate, but the land itself can't lose value.

Review these key terms:

- *Appreciation*: Value going up

- *Depreciation*: Value going down

- *Useful life*: How long an asset lasts before being replaced

- *Book value*: Value after depreciation (the original cost minus depreciation)

- *Accrued depreciation*:   Total depreciation to date (yearly depreciation times number of years)

- *Depreciation Rate*: The yearly rate times the number of years

Example

A building costs $240,000 and has a useful life of 20 years. Original Cost = $240,000; Useful Life = 20 years; Depreciation = $12,000/year ($240,000 divided by 20 years)

After two years, what is the accrued depreciation and book value?

Answer: Original Cost ($240,000) – Depreciation ($24,000) = Book Value ($216,000)

CHAPTER 6 ANSWER KEY:

1. 12.17	2. 15.08	3. 3.65
4. 2.09	5. 1.60	6. 0.122
7. 5.67	8. 5.67	9. 530.20
10. 2.0018	11. 9.76	12. 1.0
13. 3.20	14. 186.67	15. 27.83
16. 0.19	17. 0.30	18. 22.13
19. 1 ¼	20. 1 $\frac{2}{7}$	21. 2 $\frac{1}{6}$
22. 4 $\frac{2}{3}$	23. 2 11/12	24. ¼
25. $\frac{2}{3}$	26. 2	27. 1 $\frac{1}{8}$
28. $\frac{2}{3}$	29. 2 $\frac{5}{6}$	30. 3 $\frac{1}{12}$
31. $\frac{1}{8}$	32. 16	33. $\frac{8}{35}$
34. 1 $\frac{1}{3}$	35. 3 $\frac{1}{9}$	36. 6 $\frac{3}{7}$
37. 0.50	38. 1.10	39. .06
40. .254	41. 200 percent	42. 7600 percent
43. 4 percent	44. 1323 percent	45. $\frac{2}{25}$
46. $\frac{69}{200}$	47. $\frac{9}{20}$	48. $\frac{123}{100}$
49. 87.5 percent	50. 25 percent	51. 275 percent
52. 125 percent	53. $\frac{8}{25}$	54. $\frac{3}{25}$
55. $\frac{4}{5}$	56. $\frac{37}{2}$	57. .333
58. 4.25	59. 2.20	60. 0.30

61. 50,625 SF

62. 45,000 SF

63. 6,250 SF

64. 22,500 SF

65. 4,000 SF

66. 70,650 SF

67. 20,096 SF

68. 8,064 CF

69. 24.73 CF

70. 6,120 CF

71. 674 ft.

72. 20 ft.

73. 50.24 ft.

CHAPTER 7

PRACTICE TEST AND ANSWER KEY

The following sample questions are based on the national criteria and real estate regulations. Don't forget to look for your own state-specific rules and laws.

NATIONAL PRACTICE EXAM #1

1. A homeowner has $149,570.75 left to pay on the mortgage. The interest rate is 7.5 percent, and the monthly payment is $1150.00. After the next two payments, the balance will be:

   A. $149,451.30

   B. $149,355.57

   C. $149,139.04

   D. $149,570.05

2. The lender's right to call in the loan in case of default and put the secured property up for sale is based on the mortgage's:

   A. fine print

   B. equity of redemption

   C. defeasance clause

   D. acceleration clause

3. Commercial banks would rather make short-term loans like construction loans and 90-day business loans. The reason for their preference is that:

   A. The source of their lending funds is primarily from CDs.

   B. The source of their lending funds is primarily from checking accounts.

   C. The source of their lending funds is primarily from savings accounts.

   D. The source of their lending funds is primarily from issuing bonds.

4. After the sale of the collateral property, the net proceeds did not completely pay off the debt. In this situation, the borrower will probably receive a

   A. letter of defeasance

   B. notice of a deficiency judgment

   C. certificate of liability

   D. notice of foreclosure

5. FHA mortgage insurance premium is calculated at a rate of ½ percent annually. How much is the premium for the month in which the remaining principal owed is $184,694?

   A. $0.05

   B. $24.00

   C. $76.96

   D. $92.34

6. The Corcorans have a gross income of $60,000. The lender wants them to spend no more than 33 percent of their income on their housing expense. A house they can buy for $240,000 has $2,400 in annual property taxes. Homeowners insurance would cost about $400 per year. At today's interest rates, monthly payments would be $6.65 per $1,000 borrowed on a 30-year mortgage. What is the smallest amount they can expect to spend for a cash down payment?

   A. $20,000

   B. $48,000

   C. $53,940

   D. $26,970

7. What is the difference between MIP and PMI?

   A. MIP is required only on VA mortgages.

   B. PMI is the older form of mortgage insurance.

   C. PMI insures conventional mortgages, and MIP insures FHA loans.

   D. There is no difference; the two terms mean the same thing.

8. The Meningers needed two different loans to buy their first home. The loan that will have first claim on the value of the house in case of foreclosure is the one that was first

   A. recorded

   B. signed

   C. applied for

   D. satisfied

9. In a loan closing, proper signatures on the promissory note create

   A. recordation of the lien on the land records

   B. the lien on the property

   C. a nonbinding fiscal contract

   D. the indebtedness of the borrower

10. Which clause, if included in a mortgage, permits a lien recorded subsequent in time to have a superior position to the mortgage that was recorded prior in time?

   A. Subordination clause

   B. Release clause

   C. Subjective clause

   D. Superior clause

11. Express covenants that protect the grantee are found in a

    A. quitclaim deed

    B. deed of trust

    C. general warranty deed

    D. sheriff's deed

12. How may FHA insured and VA guaranteed loans be assumed?

    A. On payment of an assumption fee to the seller.

    B. Either freely or on qualification of the buyer, depending on the date of the loan.

    C. Only if the new buyer is a veteran.

    D. With guaranteed agreement of the selling broker.

13. Can a ranch contain a basement?

    A. Yes, many ranches have a downstairs level.

    B. No, ranches are built on a cement slab and do not have a true basement.

    C. Yes, one of the habitable areas is located somewhat underground.

    D. No, ranches have cellars.

14. Which of the following statements is/are true regarding the FHA (Federal Housing Authority)?

    I. FHA loans are funded by conventional lenders.

    II. FHA has a program 203b that is for one-to-four family dwellings.

    III. FHA insures loans but does not guarantee them.

    A. I only.

    B. I, II, and III.

    C. II and III only.

    D. No statement is true.

15. Land consisting of a quarter section (160 acres) is sold for $1,805 per acre. What is the total sale price?

    A. $288,800

    B. $72,200

    C. $396,000

    D. $45,125

16. A purchaser contracts for a new home for $250,000 and, after making a 10 percent down payment, applies for a fixed rate loan at the rate of 7.5 percent. At the settlement on April 10, the lender collects interest up to May 1. What is the interest charge to the buyer shown on the settlement statement?

    A. $1250.00

    B. $492.19

    C. $984.38

    D. $833.33

17. The entity that relinquishes ownership through a deed of trust mortgage foreclosure is the

    A. lender

    B. beneficiary

    C. mortgagor

    D. mortgagee

18. The purchase contract is the most important document in the sales process because

    A. it provides the road map for the closing.

    B. the agent is not guaranteed payment without it.

    C. preparing sales agreements is good for the legal business.

    D. verbal real estate contracts can only be recorded in select counties.

19. Which of the following phrases is *not* discriminatory in an advertisement to lease a nonexempt 50-unit apartment complex under the current Federal Fair Housing Act?

    A. No handicapped alteration will be made.

    B. Adults only; no children.

    C. No propane or charcoal grills on premises.

    D. Females only.

20. The purpose of RESPA is to

    A. help a buyer know how much money is required

    B. make sure that buyers do not borrow more than they can afford

    C. allow the REALTOR® to accept kickbacks from the buyer's lender

    D. see that a buyer and seller know all settlement costs

21. Important provisions of RESPA include all the following except

    A. the settlement location must be at an attorney or bank office

    B. a uniform settlement statement

    C. the lender's estimate of settlement costs

    D. the disclosure of controlled business

22. Which method of foreclosure is used in a deed of trust mortgage lien?

    A. Deed in lieu of accepted by lender

    B. Probate court ordered sale

    C. Sheriff's sale at the courthouse

    D. Non-judicial power of sale

23. Mark Stuart, a widower, died without leaving a Will or other instruction. His surviving children received ownership of his real estate holdings by

    A. adverse possession

    B. law of intestate succession

    C. beneficiary's writ

    D. eminent domain

24. An abstract of title contains

    A. the summary of a title search

    B. an attorney's opinion of title

    C. a registrar's certificate of title

    D. written opinion of title from the County Registrar's Clerk

25. A bookstore in the North Mall pays a base rent each month plus additional rent based on the amount of business it does. It is operating under a

    A. ground lease

    B. holdover lease

    C. net lease

    D. percentage lease

26. Tammi Coady lives in one side of a duplex house. She wants to advertise the other side as non-smoking. Can she legally do so?

    A. Yes, because she occupies part of the house herself.

    B. Yes, because the right to smoke is not protected by law.

    C. No, because a property owner cannot advertise discriminatory practices.

    D. No, because each housing unit is its own Book and Page number.

27. The term "walk-through" refers to

    A. the buyer's final inspection of the property to check its condition

    B. an FHA-approved termite inspection

    C. a seller's check of the premises before an open house is held

    D. an appraiser's inspection of the interior of the subject property

28. An owner who transfers real property through a Will is known as

    A. devisee

    B. legatee

    C. testator

    D. beneficiary

29. Kelly has a three-year lease on her apartment. At the end of the three years

   A. the landlord must notify her if he wants her to vacate

   B. she must give the landlord one month's notice of termination or departure

   C. the landlord must give her an option to extend at the current rent amount plus market escalation

   D. neither party need give the other any notice of termination

30. Property managers often make management decisions about tenant selection and budgets for their clients. In these relationships, the property manager is acting as a(n)

   A. subagent

   B. power of attorney

   C. general agent

   D. independent contractor

31. Net operating income (NOI) is found by

   A. subtracting yearly operating expenses from effective gross income

   B. dividing effective gross income by the cap rate

   C. subtracting yearly operating expenses from the appraiser's estimate of potential gross income

   D. multiplying effective gross income by the cap rate

32. An oral agreement between a lessor and lessee is legally

    A. a valid tenancy for one year

    B. unenforceable due to the statute of frauds

    C. unenforceable due to the statute of limitations

    D. a valid tenancy at will

33. A prospect for the lease of a commercial property feels the need for adversarial representation and hires a broker to negotiate the lease on his behalf. The contract entered into between the prospect and the broker is called

    A. an authorization to negotiate with limited Power of Attorney

    B. a cooperative brokerage agreement

    C. a property management agreement

    D. a buyer broker agreement

34. The seller of a house built before 1978 is required by law to furnish the buyer with a

    A. Good Faith Estimate (GFE) of settlement costs

    B. lead paint information booklet

    C. seller's property information disclosure

    D. proof of flood insurance

35. Rufus Chaffee hires Chris Brown, a property manager, to lease a house that he owns. Rufus is Chris's

    A. client

    B. customer

    C. fiduciary

    D. subagent

36. The responsibilities of the property manager include all of the following except

    A. maintaining the property while preserving finances

    B. marketing for a constant tenant base

    C. preparing and submitting budgets

    D. seeking interested buyers

37. The landlord has the right to access the premises

    A. in case of emergency

    B. for the purposes of making unannounced "spot" checks

    C. when the tenant is away for an extended time

    D. none of the above

38. What would you pay for a building producing $20,000 net income annually and showing a minimum rate of 8 percent?

    A. $50,000

    B. $250,000

    C. $160,000

    D. $200,000

39. The correct formula for estimating value using the cost approach is

    A. cost to reproduce + value of land = value

    B. depreciation + value of land − cost to reproduce = value

    C. value of land + cost to reproduce − depreciation = value

    D. cost to reproduce − depreciation + value of land = value

40. The right to occupy a property without interference for a specified period of time is known as a

    A. leasehold

    B. prescriptive easement

    C. trespass

    D. eminent domain

41. The Civil Rights Act of 1866 prohibits discrimination in real estate based on

    A. race

    B. race and gender

    C. handicap and country of origin

    D. whether buyer is from one of the former Confederate states

42. Market data approach appraising may require adjustments of sold comparables by an appraiser for all of the following except

    A. sale date of comparable

    B. financing made available by seller

    C. replacement cost of existing homeowner's recent improvements

    D. lot size and location

43. When an appraiser deducts depreciation using the reproduction cost of a building, the depreciation represents

    A. loss of value due to any cause

    B. costs to modernize property

    C. lack of site improvements

    D. loss of value due only to age of improvements

44. A residential property was built 105 years ago. Three of the five bed-rooms have no closets, the basement floor is heavily cracked, and the original wood shake roof needs repairs. To the appraiser, the most important consideration is

    A. how the bedrooms could be reconfigured to provide some storage

    B. how much it would cost to finish the basement floor

    C. the sale price of a nearby similar property

    D. the life expectancy of the roof

45. Assuming the NOI remains constant, what will happen to the present value of the property if the cap rate increases? The present value will

    A. increase

    B. decrease

    C. stay the same

    D. increase at first and then decrease

46. The closed sale price of an income property divided by its gross monthly rent equals the

    A. unit density ratio

    B. gross rent multiplier

    C. gross income multiplier

    D. capitalization rate

47. For appraising a 15-year-old single family house, the best data is the

    A. probable rent figure

    B. replacement cost

    C. recent sale prices of nearby houses

    D. owner's original cost plus money spent on improvements + market appreciation

48. Prices are likely to rise when there is a

    A. seller's market

    B. buyer's market

    C. thin market

    D. local employer introducing a new product line

49. What will the amount of taxes payable be if the property's assessed value is $170,000 and the tax rate is 50 mills in a community where the equalization factor is 120 percent?

    A. $12,000

    B. $10,200

    C. $3,460

    D. $8,500

50. The most profitable way in which a property can be used is known as its

    A. highest and best use

    B. plottage value

    C. condoization

    D. principle of progression

51. In the market or sales data approach of appraisal, the sales prices of similar, recently sold properties are

    A. adjusted

    B. analyzed

    C. assessed

    D. only used if the sales have occurred within the past six months

52. A single-family property located in an industrial area has a minimum value because of the principle of

    A. conformity

    B. contribution

    C. noise and air pollution

    D. diminishing returns

53. The most accurate way to uniquely locate and bound a parcel of real property is to use

    A. points that are shown on the lender's plot map

    B. a metes and bounds survey

    C. the assessor parcel number

    D. latitude and longitude bearings

54. The purchaser of a cooperative apartment receives shares in the cooperative and a

    A. bargain and sale deed

    B. proprietary lease

    C. joint tenancy

    D. limited partnership

55. A small ranch is being built on a newly acquired 25-acre parcel of land. The new owner plans to enclose the property with a chain link fence. The rectangular lot has 1,089 feet of frontage on the state road. How many feet of fencing will be needed?

    A. 2,090 feet

    B. 4,595 feet

    C. 4,270 feet

    D. 4,178 feet

56. The type of ownership that would give an investor the greatest flexibility when selling his or her interest would be

    A. a general partnership

    B. joint tenancy

    C. ownership in severalty

    D. a limited partnership

57. Of the following, which lien has the lowest property?

    A. unsecured judgment

    B. a mortgage or trust deed

    C. property taxes

    D. mechanic's lien

58. Rob has the right to cross Scott's property to get to his property. What is the right called?

    A. a right of way

    B. an easement by prescription

    C. an easement in gross

    D. an appurtenant easement

59. Mike owned fee simple title to a lot next door to a zoo. He gave the lot to the zoo as a gift. However, he wanted to make sure it would always be used for zoo purposes. His attorney prepared his deed to convey ownership of the lot to the zoo "so long as it is used for zoo purposes." The zoo owns a

   A. fee simple estate

   B. fee simple absolute

   C. fee simple determinable

   D. subordinate estate

60. An acre contains approximately

   A. 5270 square yards

   B. 45,000 square yards

   C. one quarter square mile

   D. 43,560 square feet

61. A zoning commission may grant a variance to property use when which of the following exists?

   A. limitation of feasible building sites due to land contours

   B. property improvement will be beneficial for neighborhood

   C. alternative building site that increase owner's costs

   D. over-budget development costs to a subdivider

62. Tenancy by the entirety is a special form of ownership available only to

    A. sole owners

    B. limited liability corporations

    C. married couples

    D. civil unions

63. Which of the following is not a physical characteristic of land?

    A. wetland concentration

    B. indestructibility

    C. non-homogeneity

    D. situs

64. A purchase in which the seller holds title until a specified number of payments have been made is known as a

    A. future delivery purchase

    B. deferred transfer mortgage

    C. contract for deed

    D. collateral mortgage

65. Which of the following actions is legally permitted?

    A. advertising property for sale only to a special ethnic group

    B. refusing to make a mortgage loan to a minority individual because of a poor credit history

    C. altering the terms of a loan for a member of a minority group

    D. telling a minority individual that an apartment has been rented when in fact it has not been rented

66. A deed restriction is also known as a land use covenant. Which of the following is an example of a land use covenant?

    A. minimum square footage of homes within a subdivision

    B. type of fencing constructed by owner

    C. Energy-Star fixtures within a structure

    D. Both A and B

67. A valid deed must contain

    A. a legal description

    B. a survey of the property

    C. date stamp from the County Registrar

    D. the signature of the grantee

68. An appraiser may take this factor into consideration when appraising a property

    A. familial status

    B. age of property

    C. religions of area churches

    D. race of neighborhood

69. Which is not an exemption to the Federal Housing Act?

    A. An owner who occupies a one-to-four family dwelling may limit the rental of rooms or units.

    B. Housing may be limited for use by senior citizens if occupied by one person at least 55 years of age or older.

    C. A man with two children.

    D. Religious organizations may limit the occupancy of real estate that it owns to its members if the units are not owned for business purposes.

70. Which of the following statements best describes a real estate agent's liabilities concerning environmental hazards?

  A. Residential real estate agents do not need to know about environmental conditions.

  B. Unless the buyer notices something, the real estate agent does not have to worry about it.

  C. Disclosure of environmental hazards is the responsibility of the seller.

  D. A real estate agent licensee could be liable if he or she should have known about a condition, even if the seller neglected to disclose it.

71. Which of the following would not be allowed under the Federal Housing Act?

  A. The owner of a nine-unit apartment building renting to men only.

  B. A landlord refusing to rent his double home, in which he lives, to a woman with two children and two cats.

  C. An Elks Lodge renting rooms only to members who belong to the Elks Lodge.

  D. A landlord limiting housing to persons age 62 or older.

72. When describing the particulars of a property, the agent does not disclose that a capital improvement project has been approved that will result in a special assessment to the owner in the near future. The broker has

  A. acted in accordance with the duties of a fiduciary

  B. committed fraud

  C. refrained from disclosing anything that would weaken the principal's bargaining position

  D. acted in an unethical manner, but not fraudulently

73. A broker would not be violating a law for making the statement, "This is the most beautiful harbor view in the state," because it is considered harmless

   A. puffing

   B. showmanship

   C. advertising

   D. misrepresentation

74 Agent Harris has just returned from a closing for a property that sold for $125,000. The property was listed by ABC Realty. Harris received 2 percent of the sale price total commission for the transaction from the closing agent. Harris is on a 55/45 split with his company. How much commission will Harris receive?

   A. $5,000

   B. $3,750

   C. $1,375

   D. $1,320

75. All are protected classes except

   E. a 34-year-old man

   F. national origin

   G. race

   H. handicap

76. When may a broker acting as an intermediary appoint one person to communicate with the seller and another person to communicate with the buyer?

   A. When in the judgment of the broker it is best to make such appointments.

   B. When written permission to do so has been obtained from the parties.

   C. When the parties have given verbal approvals to make such appointments, after shaking hands in agreement.

   D. When the seller has given written consent for the broker to do so.

77. When a buyer makes an offer and a seller changes a few of the terms before he signs and returns it, that is a

   A. rejection

   B. seller concession

   C. counteroffer

   D. conditional rejection

78. Which of the following listings is risky and open to dishonest dealings?

   A. listing your brother's home, under applicable guidelines

   B. a net listing

   C. an exclusive agency

   D. an exclusive right to sell

79. In a real estate transaction, a broker does not affirmatively represent either the buyer or the seller as agent. He is acting as

   A. a non-representing dual agent

   B. an undisclosed dual agent

   C. a transaction broker

   D. an illegal real estate subagent

80. Which of these would not be permitted under the Federal Fair Housing Act?

   A. The owner of a 30-unit residential apartment building renting only to black men

   B. An Arabian owner refusing to rent his home to an Israeli

   C. The USO in NY renting rooms only to service personnel

   D. An owner who lives on one side of a duplex refusing to rent to a family with five children on the other side of the duplex

81. A broker takes a sales agreement to his seller for full price. The seller states he will not accept this agreement because the buyers are Mexican. The broker should do which of the following?

   A. Abide by the principle directions and return the offer to the selling broker

   B. Explain to the owner that his refusal to sign because of the buyer's race violates federal laws

   C. Bring sales agreements to the seller from non-Mexican buyers only

   D. Tell the buyers that they'll need to find another property

82. After a purchase contract is accepted, the parties may later make additional agreements without changing the original document by use of

    A. a time extension

    B. a revision

    C. an addendum

    D. a contingency

83. The buyer has been held to be in default on a contract of sale. If buyer and seller had not agreed on liquidated damages, the seller could do which of the following?

    A. Sue the buyer for compensatory damages

    B. Obtain a court order preventing the buyer from purchasing another property

    C. Have the buyer incarcerated

    D. Only keep the buyer's earnest deposit

84. The statute of frauds requires that

    A. certain contracts, including those of real estate, must be in writing to be enforceable

    B. the seller of real estate provide a written disclosure about the condition of the property

    C. real estate brokers answer buyers' and sellers' questions honestly

    D. property deeds must be recorded in the appropriate County Registry

85. The buyer makes an offer to purchase a property and specifies that the owner accept or reject the offer within 48 hours. Before hearing back from the owner, the buyer locates a more attractive property and withdraws the offer. Is the buyer legally permitted to withdraw his offer?

   A. Yes, an offer with a condition to respond in 48 hours is not valid

   B. No, the offer is binding until the 48-hour time period expires

   C. Yes, either party may withdraw an offer or counteroffer at any time prior to its acceptance

   D. Yes, until the seller physically signs an acceptance, it is not a valid contract

86. The broker's only responsibility at the conveyance is to

   A. verify and receive the brokerage fee/commission

   B. explain the clauses found in the deed

   C. review the title report for clouds or other problems

   D. interpret the terms and conditions contained in the loan documents

87. One effect of a clause in a sales agreement that states that "time is of the essence" might be that

   A. the seller can take care of matters at their convenience

   B. the buyer must deal with the details of the contract as they occur

   C. all parties, exclusive of the agent, must attend to details quickly

   D. all parties must attend to those details called for in the agreement in a timely manner

88. At a general meeting of a brokers' trade association, several members begin talking about fees and business practices. This sort of activity could be considered

   A. a good way for brokers to learn about the different practices regionally

   B. activity endorsed by the Chamber of Commerce

   C. an appropriate activity within the association

   D. a violation of the Sherman Anti-Trust Act

89. An appraiser estimates annual rental collections on an investment property of $99,000. The vacancy factor is 5 percent and operating expenses run 25 percent of gross income. A similar investment should generate a ROI of 15 percent. Using the income approach to value, what is the market value of this property?

   A. $462,000

   B. $627,000

   C. $396,000

   D. $660,000

90. The Beans put their house on the market, the Browns made a written purchase offer, and the Beans accepted the offer in writing. When is the contract valid?

   A. Immediately.

   B. As soon as the signatures are notarized.

   C. When it is placed in the public records.

   D. When the Browns are notified of the acceptance, verbally or in writing.

91. The investor criterion for a home mortgage is an uninsured LTV ratio of 90 percent of the appraisal. The sales agreement and appraisal is in the amount of $180,000. Following underwriting guidelines, the buyer qualifies for a loan of $155,000. How much of the purchase will be financed by this investor?

    A. $162,000

    B. $135,000

    C. $108,750

    D. $155,000

92. The seller offers to pay three points on the buyer's 80 percent loan. If the house sells for $350,000, what is the expense to the seller?

    A. $10,500

    B. $2,400

    C. $3,000

    D. $8,400

93. David and Sandra Schneider have paid a total of $10,500 in mortgage interest and $1,500 in property taxes in this tax year. If they are in the 30 percent tax bracket, their tax savings is

    A. $3,600

    B. $1,000

    C. $8,400

    D. $12,000

94. The area of a lot that measures 425 feet × 425 feet is how many square yards?

    A. 26,759

    B. 120,416

    C. 40,139

    D. 361,251

95. Closing occurs on October 10. Annual property taxes of $9,000 are paid at the end of the year. What is the correct entry for the closing statement for the proration of taxes?

    A. $750

    B. $700

    C. $7,500

    D. $7,000

96. The Sherman Anti-Trust Act prohibits real estate brokers from

    A. selling each other's listings

    B. discriminating based on religion or ethnicity

    C. advertising the amount of down payment needed on a property

    D. agreeing to set standard co-broker commission rates

97. House A sold for $132,000. It had three bedrooms, two bathrooms, and a two-car garage. In the same neighborhood one month later, House B sold for $142,000. It had a three-car garage, but otherwise was similar to House A. House C (subject property) has a two-car garage. What would the appraiser adjust for the extra garage space on House B?

   A. $10,000 deduction from the value of House B

   B. $8,000 deduction from the value of House A

   C. $10,000 addition to the value of House B

   D. $8,000 addition to the value of House A

98. If a lender agrees to make a loan based on a 95 percent LTV, what is the amount of a loan for a property appraised for $135,000 and a sale price of $137,800?

   A. $130,910

   B. $105,920

   C. $128,110

   D. $128,250

99. Tom Corcoran, a property owner, just received a bill from her local taxing authority in the amount of $3,060. Property taxes in this town are based on 80 percent of an assessed value, and the rate is $1.50 per hundred. What value has the assessor placed on Tom's property?

   A. $204,000

   B. $163,200

   C. $255,000

   D. $285,000

100. What is the square footage of a living room measuring 32 feet by 23 feet?

   A. 637

   B. 906

   C. 550

   D. 736

ANSWER KEY FOR PRACTICE EXAM

1. C, $149,139.04

   Explained: $149,570.75 × 0.075 /12 = $934.82 month interest

   $1150.00- $934.82 = $215.18 principal

   $149,570.75 - $215.18 = $149,355.57

   $149,355.57 × 0.075 /12 = $933.47 month interest

   $1150.00- $933.47 = $216.53

   $149,355.57 - $216.53 = $149,139.04

2. D, acceleration clause

3. B, the source of their funds is primarily from checking accounts

4. B, notice of a deficiency judgment

5. C, $76.96

   Explained: Annual premium is $184,694 = $184,694 × .005 = $923.47

   Per month equals- $923.47 /12 = $76.96

6. D, $26,970

   Explained: Gross monthly income is $60,000 /12 = $5,000.

   33 percent of $5,000 = $1,650 for PITI.

   Subtracting monthly property taxes and H.O. Insurance equals $1,650 - $200.00 - $33.33 = $1,416.67.

   At $6.65 per $1,000, $1,416.67 will pay for $213.03, or $213,030 borrowed for their mortgage.

   $1416.67 /6.65 = $213.03.

   If they buy a home for $240,000, the buyers will need $240,000 - $213,030 = $26,970 as a down payment.

7. C, PMI insures conventional mortgages, and MIP insures FHA loans

8. A, recorded

9. D, the indebtedness of the borrower

10. A, a subordination clause

11. C, general warranty deed

12. B, either freely or on qualification of the buyer, depending on the date of the loan

13. B, ranches are built on a cement slab and do not have a true basement

14. B, I, II, and III (all); all three stipulations are true for FHA loans

15. A, $288,800; a ¼ section equals 160 acres; $1805/acre × 160 = $288,800

16. C, $984.38

    Explained: interest on new loans is collected in advance at the closing until the first of next month; $250,000 × 0.90 = $225,000

    $225,000 × 0.075 /360 days in year × 21 days = $984.38

    (Author's note — Recognize that in typical scenarios, the borrower will ALSO be required to pay a monthly mortgage insurance payment/fee for all loans over 80 percent LTV.)

17. C, mortgagor

18. A, it provides the road map for the closing

19. C, no propane or charcoal grills

20. D, see that a buyer and seller know all settlement costs

21. A, the settlement location must be at an attorney or bank office

22. D, non-judicial power of sale

23. B, law of intestate succession

24. A, the summary of a title search

25. D, percentage lease

26. B, Yes, because the right to smoke is not protected by law

27. A, the buyer's final inspection of the property to check its condition

28. C, testator

29. D, neither party need give the other any notice of termination

30. C, general agent

31. A, subtracting yearly operating expenses from effective gross income

32. D, a valid tenancy at will

33. D, a buyer broker agreement

34. B, lead-paint information booklet

35. A, client

36. D, seeking interested buyers

37. A, in case of an emergency

38. B, $250,000

    Explained: $20,000 / .08 = $250,000

39. D, cost to reproduce – depreciation + value of land = value

40. A, leasehold

41. A, race

42. C, replacement cost of existing homeowner's recent improvements

43. A, loss of value due to any cause

44. C, the sale price of a nearby similar property

45. B, decrease

46. B, gross rent multiplier

47. C, recent sale prices of nearby houses

48. A, seller's market

49. B, $10,200

    Explained: $170,000 × 1.20 = $204,000 /1,000 = 204 × 50 = $10,200

50. A, highest and best use

51. A, adjusted

52. A, conformity

53. B, a metes and bounds survey

54. B, proprietary lease

55. D, 4,178 feet

Explained: (25 acres × 43,560 square feet/acre) /1,089 front feet = 1,000 feet deep

(1,000 × 2 sides) + (1,089 × 2 sides) = 4,178 lineal feet

56. C, ownership in severalty

57. A, unsecured judgment

58. D, an appurtenant easement

59. C, fee simple determinable

60. C, 43,560 square feet

61. A, limitation of feasible building sites due to land contours

62. C, married couples

63. D, situs

64. C, contract for deed

65. B, refusing to make a mortgage loan to a minority individual because of a poor credit history

66. D, both A & B; devices and fixtures within a house/structure are not dictated by a land use covenant

67. A, a legal description

68. B, age of property

69. C, a man with two children

70. D, an RE licensee could be liable if he or she should have known about a condition, even if the seller neglected to disclose it

71. A, the owner of a nine-unit apartment building renting to men only

72. B, committed to fraud

73. A, puffing

74. C, $1,375.20

    Explained: $125,000 × 0.020 = $2,500 × 0.55 = $1,375

75. D, a 34-year-old man

76. B, when written permission to do so has been obtained from both parties

77. C, counteroffer

78. B, a net listing

79. C, a transaction broker

80. A, the owner of a 20-unit residential apartment building renting only to black men

81. B, explain to the owner that his refusal to sign because of the buyer's race violates federal laws

82. C, a revision

83. A, sue the buyer for compensatory damages

84. A, certain contracts, including those real-estate related, must be in writing to be enforceable

85. C, Yes, either party may withdraw an offer or counteroffer at any time prior to its acceptance

86. A, verify and receive the brokerage fee

87. D, all parties must attend to those details called for in the agreement in a timely manner

88. D, a violation of the Sherman Anti-Trust Act

89. A, $462,000

    Explained: $99,000 × .95 = $94,050 net income

    $99,000 × 0.25 = $24,750 operating expenses

    $94,050 - $24,750 = $69,300

    $69,300 / 0.15 = $462,000

90. D, when the Browns are notified of the acceptance either verbally or in writing

91. D, $155,000;

Explained: a loan is based upon many underwriting factors, including the LTV percent. The most restrictive (lowest) factor will be the key factor. Based solely on LTV percent, amount qualified = $180,000 × 0.90 = $162,000. This is higher than the underwriter's decision of $155,000.

92. D, $8,400

Explained: $350,000 × 0.80 = $280,000 loan amount

$280,000 × 0.03 = $8,400 = the cost of points

93. A, $3,600

Explained: $10,500 + $1,500 = $12,000 × 0.30 = $3,600

94. C, 40,139

Explained: (425 feet × 425 feet) / 9 (conversion factor) = 40,139 square yards

95. D, $7,000

Explained: $9,000 /12 = $750/month

$750 /30 = $25.00 /day for taxes

9 full months = 9 × $750 = $6,750

10 days in October = 10 × $25/day = $250

$250 + $6,750 = $7,000

96. D, agreeing to set standard co-broker commission rates

97. A, $10,000 deduction from the value of House B; per the info and comps given, the value of a garage is listed here to be $10,000

98. D, $128,250

Explained: $135,000 × .95 = $128,250 (LTV is based on the lesser of the appraised value and the sales price)

99. C, $255,000

Explained: ($3,060 /1.5) × (100 /0.80) = $255,000

100. D, 736

Explained: 32 × 23 = 736 (length × width = area)

CASE STUDY

Suzanne S.
Real Estate Sales Agent, 20+ years

I first worked as a sales agent for about 20 years, and then I got my broker's license, which I have had now for 13 years. Still, with all this time and deals, there is about one-third of the material from the exam which I have never used. I think a lot of that has to do with the brokerage that you work for and what niche of real estate you are involved in. For me, I wish they had more questions on commercial real estate, as that is the focus of my business.

The hardest part of the exam, and this was quite a while ago, was the true or false section. Though that might sound like an easy part of the test, the way the questions are worded are fairly confusing. If a statement is not 100 percent true and correct, then that statement is false. Many test-takers get hung up on that.

When I took the exam, there were not that many pre-exam prep courses or other avenues around. Courses were not mandatory, and I did not take one. I did the best I could with the help of a reference book and some other literature, and I ended up passing the exam on my first try.

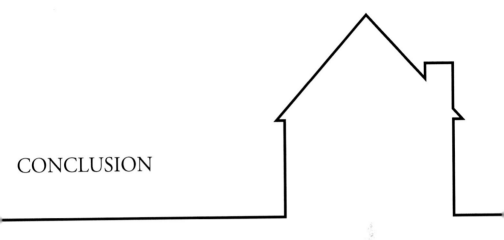

CONCLUSION

Whether you're a week or two away from taking your state's real estate salesperson license exam or it's on the distant horizon, by this point you've reviewed all of the following pieces of real estate:

- Real estate finance/mortgages
- Real estate law
- Real estate principles
- Real estate contracts and deeds
- Appraisals

You have also fully reviewed ideas about test-taking procedures and advice on decreasing anxiety and building your self-confidence before and during the test.

Don't forget to practice all the math review problems; this is a good refresher for most of us who don't use math and geometry every day. Most importantly, complete (in their entirety) the practice tests. Grade yourself and see how you do. Go back and spend more time on the questions that you didn't do well on.

It's also essential for you to approach your state or other sources to determine what needs to be known specifically in your state, in addition to the general national coursework.

For a relatively cheap price (between $25 and $30), certain exam preparation companies will allow you to take practice exams that focus exclusively on your state. Many of these online companies keep all the questions and information up-to-date, and they will give immediate scoring to see how you do. They will also provide you with the correct answers. You should print out the answers (along with their questions) and spend some time studying these as well as the information presented in this book.

For a state-by-state list of exam guidelines, see Appendix B at the end of this book. For a state-by-state list of real estate commissions, see Appendix C.

Remember, you *can* pass the exam — and on your first try too! Have confidence in yourself and in the material you have learned from this book.

Good luck!

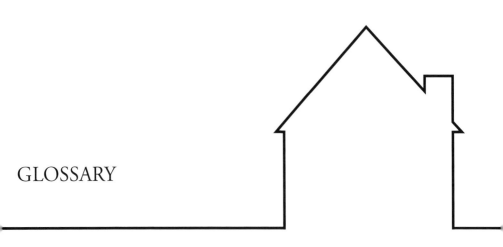

GLOSSARY

- A -

Abstract of title: A summary of the history of a title to a parcel of real estate.

Acceleration clause: A clause in a contract that gives the lender the right to demand immediate payment of the balance of the loan.

Acceptance: Agreeing to accept an offer. If one party offers to buy a property at a specific price and under specific terms, and the owner agrees to those terms, then his or her acceptance means the sales contract is complete.

Accrued items, active: Expenses prepaid within the current business year that must be imputed to the new business year. A rent prepayment entitles the company to use its rented facilities during the new business year.

Accrued items, passive: Items of expense on a closing statement that are incurred but not yet payable, such as interest on a mortgage loan or taxes on real property.

Acknowledgment: A formal declaration made before a duly authorized officer, usually a notary public, by a person who has signed a document. Documents requiring acknowledgement must be witnessed by an authorized officer like a notary public to become legal and enforceable.

Acre: The standard of measurement for property. An acre is calculated in square feet or square yards. One acre equals 4,840 square yards or 43,560 square feet.

Acreage zoning: Zoning requirements that require plans for large building lots in an effort to reduce residential or commercial density. Acreage zoning is sometimes called large-lot zoning or snob zoning.

Ad valorem: A Latin phrase which means "according to value." It refers to a tax that is imposed on a property's value, typically based on the local government's evaluation of the property.

Addendum: An addition or update for an existing contract between parties. It allows a revision to a contract without creating an entirely new contract, and it is only enforceable if both parties agree and sign.

Addition: Construction that increases a building's size or significantly adds to it. Finishing previously unfinished space is not considered an addition, but is instead considered an improvement.

Adjustable Rate Mortgage (ARM): A home loan with an interest rate that is adjusted periodically to reflect changes in a specific financial resource.

Adjustment date: The date at which the interest rate is adjusted for an Adjustable Rate Mortgage (ARM).

Adjustment period: The amount of time between adjustments for the interest rate in an Adjustable Rate Mortgage (ARM).

Advance fee: A fee paid before services are rendered. For example, a real estate broker may require an advance fee to cover advertising expenses associated with marketing the property.

Adverse possession: The actual, open, notorious, hostile, and continuous possession of another's land under a claim of title.

Affordability index: A measurement of housing affordability compiled by the NAR. The intent of the affordability index is to measure the ability of area residents to buy homes in that area.

Affordable housing: A term frequently used to describe public and private efforts to help low-income individuals purchase homes. Typical programs include below-market interest rates, easier credit terms, or minimal down payments.

Agency: The relationship between a principal and an agent wherein the agent is authorized to represent the principal in certain transactions.

Agency disclosure: A requirement in most states that says agents who act for both buyers or sellers must disclose who they are working for in the transaction. For example, a real estate agent working for the seller must provide an agency disclosure agreement notifying potential buyers that she is working on behalf of the sellers and not the buyer.

Agent: One who acts or has the power to act for another. A fiduciary relationship is created under the law of agency when a property owner, as the principal, executes a listing agreement or management contract authorizing a licensed real estate broker to be his or her agent.

Agreement of sale: A legal document the buyer and seller must approve and sign that details the price and terms in the transaction.

Alienation: The act of transferring property to another. Alienation may be voluntary, such as by gift or sale, or involuntary, as through eminent domain or adverse possession.

Alienation clause: The clause in a mortgage or deed of trust that states that the balance of the secured debt becomes immediately due and payable at the lender's option if the property is sold by the borrower. In effect, this clause prevents the borrower from assigning the debt without the lender's approval.

Americans with Disabilities Act (ADA): Addresses rights of individuals with disabilities in employment and public accommodations. It is designed to eliminate discrimination against individuals with disabilities by requiring equal access to jobs, public accommodations, government services, public transportation, and telecommunications. It also includes the design of buildings intended to serve the public.

Amortization: The usual process of paying a loan's interest and principal via scheduled monthly payments. Simply put, amortization is the gradual paying off of a debt by making periodic installment payments.

Amortization schedule: A chart or table which shows the percentage of each payment that will be applied toward principal and interest over the life of the mortgage and how the loan balance decreases until it reaches zero.

Amortization term: The number of months it will take to amortize (pay off) the loan.

Annexation: The process whereby a city expands its boundaries to include a specific geographic area. Most states require a public vote be held within the city and the area to be annexed in order to determine public approval. Annexation can also refer to the process where personal property becomes attached to real property.

Annual Percentage Rate (APR): The effective rate of interest for a loan per year. This disclosure is required by the Truth in Lending Law. The annual percentage rate is generally higher than the advertised interest rate.

Appointments: Furnishings, fixtures, or equipment found in a home or other building. The items can increase or decrease the usability or value of the property.

Appraisal: The estimate of the value of a property on the date given by a professional appraiser, usually presented in a written document.

Appraisal report: The written report presented by an appraiser regarding the value of a property. It should include a description and summary of the methods used to calculate the value of the property.

Appraised value: The dollar amount a professional appraiser assigns to the value of a property in an appraisal report.

Appreciation: An increase in the value of a home or property. Appreciation can be due to inflation, physical additions or changes, changes to market values, and other causes.

Appurtenant easement: An easement that is annexed to the ownership of one parcel and allows the owner the use of the neighbor's land.

ARM (adjustable rate mortgage) index: A number that is publicly published and used as the basis for interest rate adjustments on an ARM.

Asbestos Containing Materials (ACM): Products or materials made with asbestos. Use of ACMs has been prohibited since the early 1980s, but some older dwellings still may contain ACMs.

Assessed value: The value placed on a home, determined by a tax assessor to calculate a tax base.

Assessor: A public officer who estimates the value of a property for taxation.

Asset: A property or item of value.

Asset management: The various tasks and areas involved in managing real estate assets from the time of initial investment until the time it is sold.

Assignment: The transfer of rights and responsibilities from one party to another.

Assignment of lease: Transfer of rights to use a leased property from one leasing party to another. For example, a college student who does not need an apartment during the summer months may assign the lease to another party for that time period.

Assignment of rents: A contract that assigns rents from the tenant of a property to the mortgage lender in case of a default. Some lenders require an assignment of rents.

Assumption: The act of assuming the mortgage of a seller.

Assumption clause: A contractual provision that enables the buyer to take responsibility for the mortgage loan from the seller.

Assumption fee: A fee charged to the buyer assuming an existing loan for processing new documents and agreements.

Attorney's opinion of title: An abstract of title that an attorney has examined and has certified to be, in his or her opinion, an accurate statement of the facts concerning the property ownership. In short, the attorney has judged the title to a particular party to be good.

- B -

Bargain and sale deed: A deed that carries with it no warranties against liens or other encumbrances but does imply that the grantor has the right to convey title. The grantor may add warranties to the deed at his or her discretion. A bargain and sale deed is one in which the grantor of the deed implies to have an interest in the property but offers no warranties of clear title.

Beneficiary: A beneficiary is a person who receives or is entitled to receive the benefits resulting from certain acts. A beneficiary can be a person for whom a trust operates or on whose behalf the income from a trust estate is drawn. The term beneficiary also refers to a lender in a deed of trust loan transaction.

Betterment: An improvement to real estate. If a property owner constructs a building on a lot, the building is considered a betterment to the property.

Bill of sale: A written legal document that transfers the ownership of personal property to another party. A bill of sale does not convey title of real estate; it is only used for transferring ownership of personal property.

Board of REALTORS®: Group of real estate license holders who are members of the state and National Association of REALTORS®.

Book value: The value of a property based on its purchase amount, plus upgrades or other additions, with depreciation subtracted. Book value is typically used by corporations to show the value of properties they own.

Breach of contract: Violation of any terms or conditions in a contract without legal excuse; for example, failure to make a payment when it is due is considered a breach of contract.

Bridge loan: Mortgage financing between the end of one loan and the beginning of another loan, or a short-term loan for individuals or companies who are still seeking more permanent financing. This is frequently used during a property's construction phase and is sometimes referred to as a gap loan or a swing loan.

Broker: A person who serves as a go-between between a buyer and seller, typically for a commission.

Brokerage: The business of being a broker; usually refers to the company or organization run by a broker.

Building code: The laws set forth by the local government regarding end use of a given piece of property. These laws may dictate the design, materials used, or types of improvements that will be allowed. New construction or improvements must meet building code; adherence to requirements is determined by building inspectors.

Buyer's market: A condition where buyers have a wide choice of properties and may negotiate lower prices. Buyer's markets occur when there are more houses for sale than there are buyers. Buyer's markets can be caused by factors like overbuilding, an economic downturn, or a decrease in the local population.

- C -

Cap: A limit on how much the monthly payment or interest rate can increase in an adjustable rate mortgage. Designed to protect the borrower from large increases in the interest rate which would naturally result in large increases to the monthly payment amount.

Capital gain: The amount of excess when the net proceeds from the sale of an asset are higher than its book value. If a buyer purchases a property for $200,000 and sells it after three years for $300,000, he or she has experienced a capital gain of $100,000.

Cash flow: The net income from an investment determined by deducting all operating and fixed expenses from the gross income. If expenses exceed income, a negative cash flow results.

Caveat emptor: A Latin phrase meaning "Let the buyer beware." The buyer is responsible for inspecting the property or item and is assumed to be buying at his or her own risk.

Certificate of title: A statement of opinion on the status of the title to a parcel of real property based on an examination of specified public records; typically given by an attorney after a title search.

Chattel: Personal property. Chattel is anything owned and tangible other than real estate. Furniture, cars, jewelry, and clothing are all examples of chattel.

Class "A": A rating usually assigned to properties that will generate the maximum rent per square foot, due to superior quality or location.

Class "B": A rating usually assigned to a property that most potential tenants would find desirable but lacks certain attributes that would result in maximum rent per square foot.

Class "C": A rating usually assigned to a property that is physically acceptable but offers few amenities; as a result, the rent per square foot will be low.

Closing: The final act of procuring a loan and title in which documents are signed between the buyer and seller, or their respective representation, and all money and consideration changes hands.

Closing costs: Expenses related to the sale of real estate including the loan, title, and appraisal fees; does not include the price of the property itself.

Closing statement: Detailed cash accounting of a real estate transaction showing all cash received, all charges and credits made, and all cash paid out because of the transaction; often, this is presented via a "HUD-1 Settlement Statement."

Code of ethics: A written system of standards for ethical conduct. For example, all REALTORS® are required to follow a code of ethics that defines professional behavior.

Collateral: The property for which a borrower has obtained a loan, thereby assuming the risk of losing the property if the loan is not repaid according to the terms of the loan agreement.

Collection: The effort on the part of a lender, due to a borrower's defaulting on a loan, which involves mailing and recording certain documents if the foreclosure procedure must be implemented.

Commercial property: Property designed for use by retail, wholesale, office, hotel, or other service businesses. Commercial properties are typically not long-term residential structures.

Commission: Payment to a broker for services rendered, such as in the sale or purchase of real property — usually a percentage of the selling price of the property.

Common Area Maintenance (CAM): Charges (over and above rent) to tenants for expenses to maintain hallways, restrooms, parking lots, playgrounds, and other common areas.

Comparables: Properties used in an appraisal report that are substantially equivalent to the subject property.

Competitive Market Analysis (CMA): A comparison of the prices of recently sold homes similar to a listing seller's home in terms of location, style, and amenities. This is also known as a comparative market analysis.

Concessions: Cash, or the equivalent, that the landlord pays or allows in the form of rental abatement, additional tenant finish allowance, moving expenses, or other costs expended to persuade a tenant to sign a lease.

Condemnation: A government agency's act of taking private property, without the owner's consent, for public use through the power of eminent domain.

Construction loan: A short-term loan to finance the cost of construction, usually dispensed in stages throughout the construction project. Most construction loans provide for periodic payouts as stages of construction completion are reached.

Consumer Price Index (CPI): A measurement of inflation relating to the change in the prices of goods and services that are regularly purchased by a specific population during a certain period of time.

Contingency: A provision or provisions in a contract that must be met for the contract to be considered enforceable. For example, a buyer may offer a contract that is contingent upon the buyer's obtaining suitable financing; if financing is not obtained, the buyer may back out of the agreement without penalty.

Contract for deed: An agreement to sell real estate by installment. The buyer may use, occupy, and enjoy the land, but no deed is given until all or a specified part of the sale price has been paid, usually in installments (monthly payments).

Contractor: A person or company who contracts to supply goods or services, generally regarding the development of a property.

Controlled business arrangement (CBA): An arrangement where a package of services (such as a real estate firm, title insurance company, mortgage broker, and home inspection company) is offered to consumers.

Conversion: Changing property to a different use or form of ownership. For example, an apartment building can be converted to condominiums, or a large residence can be converted to a multi-tenant apartment building.

Conveyance: A term used to refer to any document that transfers title to real property. The term is also used in describing the act of transferring. It's also known as closing.

Cooperative: Also called a co-op. Cooperatives are a type of ownership by multiple residents of a multi-unit housing complex, in which they all own shares in the cooperative corporation that owns the property and have the right to occupy a particular apartment or unit.

Counteroffer: A new offer made in response to an offer received. It has the effect of rejecting the original offer, which cannot be accepted thereafter unless revived by the offeror.

Covenant: A written agreement between two or more parties in which a party or parties pledge to perform or not perform specified acts regarding property; usually found in such real estate documents as deeds, mortgages, leases, and contracts for deed.

Credit: An agreement in which a borrower promises to repay the lender later and receives something of value in exchange.

Credit history: An individual's record which details his or her current and past financial obligations and performance.

Credit rating: The degree of creditworthiness a person is assigned based on his or her credit history and current financial status.

Credit report: An individual's record detailing credit, employment, and residence history used to determine the individual's creditworthiness.

Credit score: Sometimes called a Credit Risk Score (or a FICO score). A credit score is the number listed on a consumer credit report that represents a statistical summary of the information.

Creditor: A party to whom other parties owe money.

- D -

Damages: The amount recoverable by a person who has been injured in any manner, including physical harm, property damage, or violated rights, through the act or default of another. For example, a landlord whose apartment has been damaged by a tenant will seek monetary damages.

Debt-to-income ratio (DTI): The percentage of a borrower's monthly payment on long-term debts divided by his or her gross monthly income.

Deed: A legal document that conveys property ownership to the buyer. The seller delivers a deed to the buyer after the transaction (including the exchange of funds) has been completed.

Deed in trust: An instrument that grants a trustee under a land trust full power to sell, mortgage, and subdivide a parcel of real estate. The beneficiary controls the trustee's use of these powers under the provisions of the trust agreement. A provision that allows a lender to foreclose on a property if the borrower defaults on the loan.

Deed of trust: An instrument used in some states instead of a mortgage. Legal title to the property is vested in one or more trustees to secure the repayment of a loan. The deed of trust allows the lender to regain possession in case of default.

Deed restrictions: Clauses in a deed limiting the future uses of the property. Deed restrictions may impose a vast variety of limitations and conditions. For example, they may limit the density of buildings, dictate the types of structures that can be erected, or prevent buildings from being used for specific purposes or even from being used at all.

Default: The state that occurs when a borrower fails to fulfill a duty or take care of an obligation, such as making monthly mortgage payments. Not fulfilling conditions of a contract causes the party to be in default.

Deficiency judgment: A personal judgment levied against the borrower when a foreclosure sale does not produce sufficient funds to pay the mortgage debt in full.

Density: The intensity of land use. For example, if a subdivision has 20 homes in a 20-acre area, the density is one dwelling unit per acre.

Department of Housing and Urban Development (HUD): Government agency that implements and oversees federal housing and community development programs including the FHA. The HUD attempts to assure decent, safe, and sanitary housing, and investigates complaints of discrimination in housing.

Developer: One who attempts to put land to its most profitable use through the construction of improvements. A person creating a subdivision is a developer.

Devise: The gift of real property by Will. The donor (giver) is the devisor and the recipient is the devisee.

Disclosure: A written statement, presented to a potential buyer, that lists information relevant to a piece of property, whether positive or negative.

Doing Business As (DBA): Used to identify a trade name or a fictitious business name. A company using the designation DBA is not attempting to mislead or defraud customers.

Down payment: The difference between the purchase price and the portion that the mortgage lender financed. A down payment typically refers to the amount of cash a borrower puts down on the house.

Dual agency: An individual or company representing both parties to a transaction. Dual agencies are unethical (unless both parties agree) and are illegal in many states.

Duress: Unlawful constraint or action exercised upon a person whereby the person is forced to perform an act against his or her will; a compulsion to do something because of a threat. This kind of contract is voidable.

- E -

Earnest money: Money, deposited by a buyer under the terms of a contract, to be forfeited if the buyer defaults or applied to the purchase price if the sale is closed.

Easement: The right given to a non-ownership party to use a certain part of the property for specified purposes, such as servicing power lines or cable lines.

Effective gross income: The potential gross income of an income property, minus a vacancy and collection allowance.

Eminent domain: The power of the government to pay the fair market value for a property, appropriating it for public use.

Encumbrance: Anything — such as a mortgage, tax, judgment lien, easement, restriction on the use of the land, or an outstanding dower right — that may diminish the value or enjoyment of a property.

Entity: A person or corporation that is recognized by law.

Environmental Protection Agency (EPA): The agency of the United States government that enforces federal pollution laws and implements pollution prevention programs.

Equity: The value of a property after existing liabilities have been deducted, or the value of a property over and above all liens against it. A property worth $400,000 with loans totaling $300,000 against it has an equity of $100,000.

Equity of redemption: The right of an owner to reclaim property before a foreclosure sale. If the owner can raise enough funds to pay principal, interest, and taxes on the property, he can reclaim the property before a foreclosure sale, even though foreclosure proceedings may be under way.

Escrow: The closing of a transaction through a third party called an escrow agent who receives certain funds and documents to be delivered upon the performance of certain conditions outlined in the escrow instructions. Money, documents, or valuable items deposited with a third party for delivery upon the fulfillment of a condition.

Escrow account: An account established by a mortgage lender or servicing company for the purpose of holding funds for the payment of items, such as homeowners insurance and property taxes. This is also referred to as an impound account.

Estate: The total assets, including property, of an individual after he or she has died.

Estate in land: The degree, quantity, nature, and extent of interest a person has in real property.

Eviction: The legal removal of an occupant from a piece of property.

Exchange: A transaction in which all or part of the consideration is the transfer of like-kind property (such as real estate for real estate).

Execute: To sign a contract; to perform a contract fully.

Executed contract: An agreement in which all parties involved have fulfilled their duties.

Executor: The individual who is named in a Will to administer an estate. "Executrix" is the feminine form.

Extension: An agreement between two parties to extend the time period specified in a contract. Both parties must agree.

- F -

Fair Credit Reporting Act (FCRA): The federal legislation that governs the processes credit reporting agencies must follow.

Fair Housing Act: The federal law that prohibits discrimination in housing based on race, color, religion, sex, handicap, familial status, and national origin.

Fair market value: The highest price that a buyer would be willing to pay, and the lowest price a seller would be willing to accept.

Fannie Mae: Federal National Mortgage Association. A quasi-government agency established to purchase any kind of mortgage loans in the secondary mortgage market from the primary lenders.

Fannie Mae Community Home Buyers Program: A community lending model based on borrower income in which mortgage insurers and Fannie Mae offer flexible underwriting guidelines to increase the buying power for a low- or moderate-income family and to decrease the total amount of cash needed to purchase a home.

Federal Deposit Insurance Corporation (FDIC): An independent federal agency that insures the deposits in commercial banks.

Federal Emergency Management Agency (FEMA): Among other duties, offers flood insurance to property owners in designated flood plains.

Federal Home Loan Mortgage Corporation (FHLMC): A government agency also known as Freddie Mac. It buys mortgages from lending institutions, combines them with other loans, and sells shares to investors.

Federal Housing Administration (FHA): A government agency that administers many loan programs, loan guarantee programs, and loan insurance programs designed to make housing more available.

Federal National Mortgage Association (FNMA): A government agency also known as Fannie Mae. It's the nation's largest supplier of home mortgage funds. The company buys mortgages from lenders and resells them as securities on the secondary mortgage market.

Fee simple: The highest interest in real estate recognized by the law; the holder is entitled to all rights to the property.

Feudal system: A system of ownership usually associated with pre-colonial England, in which the king or other sovereign is the source of all rights. The right to possess real property was granted by the sovereign to an individual as a life estate only. Upon the death of the individual, title passed back to the sovereign, not to the decedent's heirs.

FHA loan: A loan insured by the Federal Housing Administration and made by an approved lender in accordance with the FHA's regulations.

Fiduciary relationship: A relationship of trust and confidence, as between trustee and beneficiary, attorney and client, or principal and agent.

Finance charge: The amount of interest to be paid on a loan or credit card balance.

Fixed rate: An interest rate that does not change over the life of the loan.

Fixture: An item of personal property that has been converted to real property by being permanently affixed.

Flip: Purchase and immediately resell property at a quick profit.

Flood insurance: A policy that is required in designated flood zones to protect against loss due to flood damage.

For Sale By Owner (FSBO): A method of selling property in which the property owner serves as the selling agent and directly handles the sales process with the buyer or buyer's agent.

Foreclosure: A legal procedure whereby property used as security for a debt is sold to satisfy the debt in the event of default in payment of the mortgage note or default of other terms in the mortgage document.

Frontage: The portion of a lot along a lake, river, street, or highway.

- G -

General warranty deed: A deed in which the grantor fully warrants good clear title to the premises. Used in most real estate deed transfers, a general warranty deed offers the greatest protection of any deed.

Good Faith Estimate (GFE): A lender's or broker's estimate that shows all costs associated with obtaining a home loan including loan processing, title, and inspection fees.

Government National Mortgage Association (GNMA): Also known as Ginnie Mae, this is a government-owned corporation under the U.S. Department of Housing and Urban Development (HUD) which performs the same role as Fannie Mae and Freddie Mac in providing funds to lenders for making home loans, but only purchases loans that are backed by the federal government through FHA and VA loans.

Government survey method: The system of land description that applies to most of the land in the United States, particularly the western half.

Grade: The elevation of a hill, road, sidewalk, or slope showing its inclination from level ground. Usually expressed as a percentage of level distance. For example, a 10 percent grade rises 10 feet in each 100 feet of level distance.

Grant: The term used to indicate a transfer of property. A person can grant property to another person in a deed.

GRI: Stands for Graduate, REALTOR® Institute. Denotes a person who has completed prescribed courses in law, finance, investment, appraisal, and salesmanship.

Gross income: The total income of a household before taxes or expenses have been subtracted.

Gross income multiplier: A figure used as a multiplier of the gross annual income of a property to produce an estimate of the property's value.

Gross Rent Multiplier (GRM): The figure used as a multiplier of the gross monthly income of a property to produce an estimate of the property's value.

Ground lease: A lease of land only, on which the tenant usually owns a building or is required to build as specified in the lease. Such leases are usually long-term net leases; the tenant's rights and obligations continue until the lease expires or is terminated through default.

Guardian: An individual appointed by the court to oversee and administer the personal affairs and property of an individual incapable of those duties; for example, an orphaned child.

- H -

Hearing: A formal procedure with issues of fact or law to be tried and settled. It is similar to a trial and can result in a final order.

Highest and best use: The reasonable, probable, and legal use of vacant land or an improved property that is physically possible, appropriately supported, financially feasible, and that results in the highest value.

Home Equity Conversion Mortgage (HECM): Also referred to as a Reverse Annuity Mortgage. A type of mortgage in which the lender makes payments to the owner, thereby enabling older homeowners to convert equity in their homes into cash in the form of monthly payments.

Home equity line: An open-ended amount of credit based on the equity a homeowner has accumulated.

Home equity loan: A loan (sometimes called a line of credit) under which a property owner uses his or her residence as collateral and can then draw funds up to a prearranged amount against the property.

Homeowners Association (HOA): A group that governs a community, condominium building, or neighborhood and enforces the covenants, conditions, and restrictions set by the developer.

Homestead: Land that is owned and occupied as the family home. In many states, a portion of the area or value of this land is protected or exempt from judgments for debts.

Housing Expense Ratio (HER): The percentage of gross income that is devoted to housing costs each month.

HUD-1 Settlement Statement: Also known as the closing statement or settlement sheet. An itemized listing of the funds paid at closing.

HVAC: An acronym for heating, ventilating, and air conditioning.

- I -

Income approach: The process of estimating the value of an income-producing property through capitalization of the annual net income expected to be produced by the property during its remaining useful life.

Income property: A particular property that is used to generate income but is not occupied by the owner.

Income statement: A historical financial report indicating the sources and amounts of revenues, amounts of expenses, and profits or losses. It can be prepared on an accrual or a cash basis.

Independent contractor: Someone who is retained to perform a certain act but who is subject to the control and direction of another only as to the end result and not as to the way in which the act is performed. Unlike an employee, an independent contractor pays for all expenses and Social Security and income taxes and receives no employee benefits. Most real estate salespeople are independent contractors.

Index: A financial table that lenders use for calculating interest rates on ARMs.

Instrument: A written legal document created to establish the rights and liabilities of the parties to it.

Interest: A charge made by a lender for the use of money; the cost for the use of money.

Interest rate: The percentage that is charged for a loan.

International Building Code (IBC): The standard building codes and regulations adopted by the United States since 2000.

Investment property: A piece of real estate that generates some form of income.

- J -

Joint tenancy: A form of ownership in which two or more people have equal shares in a piece of property, and rights pass to the surviving owner(s) in the event of death.

- L -

Land contract: An installment contract for sale with the buyer receiving equitable title (a right to possession) and the seller retaining legal title. This is similar to a contract for deed.

Land description: Legal description of a particular piece of real estate.

Landlord: A person or company who rents property to another person; a landlord is the lessor.

Lease: A written or oral contract between a landlord (the lessor) and a tenant (the lessee) that transfers the right to exclusive possession and use of the landlord's real property to the lessee for a specified period of time and for a stated consideration (rent).

Lease option: A financing option that provides for homebuyers to lease a home with an option to buy, with part of the rental payments being applied toward the down payment.

Lease purchase: The purchase of real property, the consummation of which is preceded by a lease, usually long-term. This is typically used for tax or financing purposes.

Legal description: A description of a specific parcel of real estate complete enough for an independent surveyor to locate and identify it.

Legatee: A person who receives property by Will.

Lessee: A person to whom property is rented under a lease.

Lessor: A person who rents property to another under a lease.

Let: To rent property to a tenant.

Liabilities: A borrower's debts and financial obligations, whether long or short-term.

Liability insurance: A type of policy that protects owners against negligence, personal injury, or property damage claims.

Lien: A claim put on property, making it security for payment of a debt, judgment, mortgage, or taxes.

Limited power of attorney: A power of attorney that is limited to a specific task or set of tasks. It does not confer general authority to act on the behalf of another party.

Liquidated damages: An amount predetermined by the parties to a contract as the total compensation to an injured party should the other party breach the contract.

Listing agreement: An agreement between a property owner and a real estate broker which authorizes the broker to attempt to sell or lease the property at a specified price and terms in return for a commission or other compensation.

Listing broker: The listing broker is the broker in a multiple-listing situation from whose office a listing agreement is initiated. The listing broker and the cooperating broker may be the same person.

Loan officer: An official representative of a lending institution who is authorized to act on behalf of the lender within specified limits.

Loan-to-value ratio (LTV): The relationship between the amount of the mortgage loan and the value of the real estate being pledged as collateral.

London Interbank Offered Rate (LIBOR): An index used to determine interest rate changes for adjustable rate mortgages. Very popular index for interest only mortgage programs.

Long-term lease: A rental agreement that will last at least three years from initial signing to the date of expiration or renewal.

- M -

Management agreement: A contract between the owner of income property and a management firm or individual property manager that outlines the scope of the manager's authority.

Market conditions: Features of the marketplace including interest rates, employment levels, demographics, vacancy rates, and absorption rates.

Market data approach: An estimate of value obtained by comparing property being appraised with recently sold comparable properties.

Market value: The price a property would sell for at a particular time in a competitive market.

Mile: 1,760 yards or 5,280 feet.

Mobile home: A dwelling unit manufactured in a factory and designed to be transported to a site and semi-permanently attached.

Monument: A fixed natural or artificial object used to establish real estate boundaries for a metes-and-bounds description.

Mortgage: An amount of money that is borrowed to purchase a property, using that property as collateral.

Mortgage broker: An individual who matches prospective borrowers with lenders that the broker is approved to deal with.

Mortgage Guaranty Insurance Corporation (MGIC): A private mortgage insurer, also known as Maggie Mae, which insures mortgages to other investors by protecting them from credit losses and expediting home ownership with low down-payment loans.

Mortgage Insurance (MI): A policy, required by lenders on some loans, that covers the lender against certain losses that are incurred because of a default on a home loan.

Mortgage Insurance Premium (MIP): The amount charged for mortgage insurance, either to a government agency or to a private MI company.

Mortgagor: The borrower (person receiving the money) in a mortgage loan transaction.

Multiple listing: An arrangement among a group of real estate brokers who agree in advance to provide information about some or all of their listings to the others, and who agree that commissions on sales of those listings will be split between listing and selling brokers.

Multiple Listing Service (MLS): A marketing organization composed of member brokers who agree to share their listing agreements with one another in the hope of procuring ready, willing, and able buyers for their properties more quickly than they could on their own. Most multiple-listing services accept exclusive-right-to-sell or exclusive-agency listings from their member brokers.

- N -

National Association of REALTORS® (NAR): An organization of REAL-TORS® devoted to encouraging professionalism in real estate activities.

Net income: The monetary sum arrived at after deducting expenses from a business or investment but before deducting depreciation expenses.

Net lease: A lease requiring the tenant to pay not only rent but also costs incurred in maintaining the property, including taxes, insurance, utilities, and repairs.

Net Operating Income (NOI): The pre-tax figure of gross revenue minus operating expenses and an allowance for expected vacancy.

Notary public: An officer who is authorized to take acknowledgements to certain types of contracts, like deeds, contracts, and mortgages, and before whom affidavits may be sworn.

- O -

Offer: A term that describes a specified price or spread to sell whole loans or securities; an expression of willingness to purchase a property at a specified price or of willingness to sell.

Offer and acceptance: Two essential components of a valid contract; a "meeting of the minds"; creates an agreement of sale.

Open house: A method of showing a house for sale where the home is left open for inspection by interested parties. Typically, a salesperson or broker is present.

Open listing: A listing contract under which the broker's commission is contingent on the broker's producing a ready, willing, and able buyer before the property is sold by the seller or another broker.

Operating expense: The regular costs associated with operating and managing a property.

Opinion of title: An opinion from an attorney, generally in certificate form, as to the validity of the title to the property being sold. It is also called a title abstract.

Ordinance: Municipal rules governing the use of land.

- P -

Paper: A business term referring to a mortgage, note, or contract for deed, usually taken back from the buyer by a seller when real property is sold.

Parcel: A specific portion of a larger tract; a lot.

Parties: Principals in a transaction or judicial proceeding. A buyer and a seller are the principals in a sales contract, while a broker is not.

Percentage lease: A lease, commonly used for commercial property, whose rental is based on the tenant's gross sales at the premises; it usually stipulates a base monthly rental plus a percentage of any gross sales above a certain amount.

Personal property: Any items belonging to a person that is not real estate; property that is movable and not fixed to land; also known as chattels.

Planned unit development (PUD): A type of ownership where individuals own the building or unit they live in, but common areas are owned jointly with the other members of the development or association. Contrasts with condominiums, where an individual owns the airspace of his unit, but the buildings and common areas are owned jointly with the others in the development or association.

Plat: A chart or map of a certain area showing the boundaries of individual lots, streets, and easements.

Point: A fee a lender charges to provide a lower interest rate, equal to one percent of the amount of the loan. It is also referred to as a discount point.

Power of attorney: A written instrument authorizing a person (who becomes the attorney-in-fact) to act as agent for another person to the extent indicated in the instrument.

Premises: Land and tenements; an estate; the subject matter of a conveyance.

Premium: The cost of an insurance policy; the value of a mortgage or bond in excess of its face amount; the amount over market value paid for some exceptional quality or feature.

Prepayment: The money that is paid to reduce the principal balance of a loan before the date it is due.

Principal, interest, taxes, insurance (PITI): The items that are included in the monthly payment to the lender for an impounded loan, as well as mortgage insurance.

Private mortgage insurance (PMI): Insurance provided by a private carrier that protects a lender against a loss in the event of a foreclosure and deficiency. This is typically required when the loan amount exceeds 80 percent of the home's value.

Probate: A legal process by which a court determines who will inherit a decedent's property and what the estate's assets are.

Promissory note: A written agreement to repay the specific amount over a certain period of time.

Property: The rights or interests an individual has in land or goods to the exclusion of all other parties; rights gained from the ownership of wealth.

Property manager: Someone who manages real estate for another person for compensation. Duties include collecting rents, maintaining the property, and keeping up all accounting.

Property tax: The tax that must be paid on private property, not on real property like real estate.

Proration: Expenses that are allocated between the seller and the buyer; expenses that are either prepaid or paid in arrears that are divided or distributed between buyer and seller at the closing.

Prospect: A person considered likely to buy.

Purchase and sale (P&S) agreement: The written contract the buyer and seller both sign defining the terms and conditions under which a property is sold.

- Q -

Qualification: Reviewing a borrower's credit and payment capacity before approving a loan.

Quitclaim deed: A written document that releases a party from any interest they may have in a property. In real estate terms, this is a conveyance by which the grantor transfers whatever interest he or she has in the real estate without warranties or obligations.

- R -

Real estate: Land and everything attached to it; the activities concerned with ownership and transfer of physical property.

Real estate agent: An individual who is licensed to negotiate and transact real estate sales.

Real estate investment trust (REIT): Trust ownership of real estate by a group of individuals who purchase certificates of ownership in the trust, which in turn invests the money in real property and distributes the profits back to the investors free of corporate income tax.

Real estate owned (REO): The real estate that a savings institution owns because of foreclosure on borrowers in default; properties that did not sell at foreclosure auction and have reverted to ownership by the lender.

Real Estate Settlement Procedures Act (RESPA): The federal law that requires certain disclosures to consumers about mortgage loan settlements. The law also prohibits the payment or receipt of kickbacks and certain kinds of referral fees. It also requires lenders to notify borrowers regarding closing costs in advance.

Real property: The interests, benefits, and rights inherent in real estate ownership; land and anything else of a permanent nature that is affixed to the land.

REALTOR®: A registered trademark term reserved for the sole use of active members of local REALTOR® boards affiliated with the National Association of REALTORS®.

Recording: The act of entering or recording documents affecting or conveying interests in real estate in the recorder's office established in each county. Until it is recorded, a deed or mortgage ordinarily is not effective against subsequent purchasers or mortgagees; the documentation that the registrar's office keeps of the details of properly executed legal documents.

Redlining: An illegal practice of a lender who refuses to make home loans in certain areas, regardless of the qualifications of prospective borrowers.

Refinance: To replace an old loan with a new loan; to pay off one loan with the proceeds from another loan.

Registrar: The person who maintains accurate and official records like deeds, mortgages, and other recorded documents.

Regulation: A rule or order prescribed for management or government. Regulations frequently have the force and effect of law.

Regulation Z: A federal legislation under the Truth in Lending Act that requires lenders to advise the borrower in writing of all costs that are associated with the credit portion of a financial transaction.

Release: To free real estate from a mortgage. This is also known as a release of lien.

Rent: The fee paid for the occupancy or use of any rental property or equipment.

Replacement cost: The projected cost by current standards of constructing a building that is equivalent to the building being appraised.

Reproduction cost: The construction cost at current prices of an exact duplicate of the subject property.

Request for proposal (RFP): A formal request that invites investment managers to submit information regarding investment strategies, historical investment performance, current investment opportunities, investment management fees, and other pension fund client relationships used by their firm.

Rescission: The practice of one party's canceling or terminating a contract, which has the effect of returning the parties to their original positions before the contract was made.

Right of first refusal: A lease clause that gives a tenant the first opportunity to buy a property or to lease additional space in a property at the same price and terms as those contained in an offer from a third-party that the owner has expressed a willingness to accept.

Right of way: The right given by one landowner to another to pass over the land, construct a roadway, or use as a pathway, without actually transferring ownership.

Right to use: The legal right to use or occupy a property.

- S -

Sale and leaseback: A transaction in which an owner sells his or her improved property and, as part of the same transaction, signs a long-term lease to remain in possession of the premises.

Sales comparison approach: The process of estimating the value of a property by examining and comparing actual sales of comparable properties.

Second mortgage: A secondary loan obtained upon a piece of property; a subordinated lien created over a mortgage loan.

Security deposit: A payment by a tenant, held by the landlord during the lease term, and kept (wholly or partially) on default or on destruction of the premises by the tenant.

Seller financing: A debt instrument taken by the seller to provide financing to a buyer.

Seller's market: Economic conditions that favor sellers, due to circumstances like a scarcity of supply or excessive demand.

Selling broker: The licensed real estate broker that finds or brings forth the buyer.

Settlement: The same as closing; the act of adjusting and prorating the credits and charges to conclude a real estate transaction.

Site: A plot of land prepared for or underlying a structure or development; the location of a property.

Slab: The flat, exposed surface that is laid over the structural support beams to form the floor of a building.

Spec ("speculative") home: A single family dwelling constructed in anticipation of finding a buyer. A spec home is built by a contractor in hopes of finding a buyer, and not due to a contract already reached with a buyer to build the home.

Special assessment: A tax or levy customarily imposed against only those specific parcels of real estate that will benefit from a proposed public improvement like a street or sewer.

Special warranty deed: A deed in which the grantor warrants, or guarantees, the title only against defects arising during the period of his or her tenure and ownership of the property and not against defects existing before that time, generally using the language, "by, through, or under the grantor but not otherwise."

Statute: A law established by an act of legislature.

Statute of limitations: The law pertaining to the period of time within which certain actions must be brought to court.

Structure: Any constructed improvement to a site. This may include buildings, fences, garages, sheds, or utility buildings.

Subagent: One who is employed by a person already acting as an agent. This term is typically referencing a salesperson licensed under a broker (agent) who is employed under the terms of a listing agreement.

Subdivision: A tract of land divided by the owner — known as the sub-divider — into blocks, building lots, and streets according to a recorded subdivision plat, which must comply with local ordinances and regulations.

Sublease: A lease from a lessee to another lessee. The new lessee becomes a sublessee or tenant.

Subletting: Leasing a premise by a lessee to a third party for part of the lessee's remaining term. Also known as subleasing.

Subordination: The act of sharing credit loss risk at varying rates among two or more classes of securities; relegation to a lesser position, usually in respect to a right or security.

Subordination clause: A clause or document that permits a mortgage recorded at a later date to take priority over an existing mortgage.

Supply and demand: The appraisal principle that follows the interrelationship of the supply of and demand for real estate. As appraising is based on economic concepts, this principle recognizes that real property is subject to the influences of the marketplace just as is any other commodity.

Survey: The process by which boundaries are measured and land areas are determined; the on-site measurement of lot lines, dimensions, and position of a house on a lot — including the determination of any existing encroachments or easements.

- T -

Tax deed: An instrument, similar to a certificate of sale, given to a purchaser at a tax sale. See certificate of sale.

Tax rate: The ratio of a tax assessment to the amount being taxed. The tax rate is established according to assessed valuations.

Tenancy at will: A license to use or occupy lands and buildings at the will of the owner. The tenant may leave the property at any time, or the owner may require the tenant to leave at any time.

Tenant: One who holds or possesses lands or tenements by any kind of right or title; also called a lessee.

Tenant improvement (TI): The upgrades or repairs that are made to the leased premises by or for a tenant.

Termite inspection: An examination of a structure by a qualified person to determine the existence of termite infestation. Most sales contracts as well as an FHA-backed loan will require a termite inspection.

Thin market: A real estate market where there are few buyers and sellers and a slow rate of turnover of properties. This is also called a limited market.

Third party: A person who is not directly involved in a transaction or contract but may be involved or affected by it.

Timeshare: A form of ownership involving purchasing a specific period of time or percentage of interest in a vacation property.

Timeshare ownership plan (TSO): A form of timesharing in which a number of individuals hold title to a particular unit as tenants in common, entitling each to use the property at specified times during the year.

Title: The right to or ownership of land; the evidence of ownership of land.

Title insurance: A policy insuring the owner or mortgagee against loss due to defects in the title to a parcel of real estate, other than encumbrances, defects, and matters specifically excluded by the policy.

Title report: A preliminary report indicating the current state of the title. It does not describe the chain of title.

Title search: The process of analyzing all transactions existing in the public record to determine whether any title defects could interfere with the clear transfer of property ownership.

Township: The principal unit of the rectangular (government) survey system. A township is a square with six-mile sides and an area of 36 square miles.

Track record: A developer or builder's reputation for producing on a timely and economical basis; the history of a real estate salesperson or broker's sales performance.

Trade fixture: Any personal property that is attached to a structure and used in the business but is removable once the lease is terminated.

Transfer tax: An amount specified by state or local authorities when ownership in a piece of property changes hands.

Triple net lease (NNN): A lease that requires the tenant to pay all property expenses on top of the rental payments.

Trust deed: An instrument used to create a mortgage lien by which the borrower conveys title to a trustee, who holds it as security for the benefit of the note holder (the lender). This is also called a deed of trust.

Truth in lending: The federal legislation requiring lenders to disclose the terms and conditions of a mortgage in writing.

- U -

Underwriting: The process during which lenders analyze the risks a particular borrower presents and set appropriate conditions for the loan.

Uniform Residential Appraisal Report (URAR): A standard form for reporting the appraisal of a dwelling. The URAR is required by major secondary mortgage purchases and includes checklists and definitions printed on the form.

Uniform Settlement Statement: A special HUD form that itemizes all charges to be paid by a borrower and seller in connection with the settlement (usually a HUD-1 form).

Unit: A suite of rooms making up a residence for one tenant. A unit generally has a separate entrance.

Useful life: The economic period during which a cash flow is expected; the period to depreciate a building for tax purposes.

Utilities: Services like water, sewer, electricity, telephone, and gas that are generally required to operate a building or a residence. Also used to describe the charges for utility services.

- V -

Vacancy factor: The percentage of gross revenue that pro forma income statements expect to be lost due to vacancies.

Vacate: To move out.

Valid contract: A contract that complies with all the essentials of a contract and is binding and enforceable on all parties.

Variable rate: The interest rate on a loan that varies over the term of the loan according to a predetermined index. This also called an adjustable rate mortgage.

Variance: Permission obtained from zoning authorities to build a structure or conduct a use that is expressly prohibited by the current zoning laws; an exception from the zoning ordinances.

Verification of Deposit (VOD): The confirmation statement a borrower's bank may be asked to sign to verify the borrower's account balances and history.

Verification of Employment (VOE): The confirmation statement a borrower's employer may be asked to sign to verify the borrower's position and salary.

Veterans Administration (VA): The federal government agency that assists veterans in purchasing a home without a down payment. In general, a veteran who has served more than 120 days active duty is eligible for a home loan with no down payment.

- W -

Waiver: The voluntary renunciation, abandonment, or surrender of a claim, right, or privilege.

Warranty: A promise contained in a contract; a promise that certain stated facts are true.

Warranty deed: A deed that contains a covenant that the grantor will protect the grantee against all claims.

Will: A written document, properly witnessed, providing for the transfer of title to property owned by the deceased, called the testator.

- X Y Z -

Zoning: The act of dividing a city or town into areas and applying laws and regulations regarding the architectural design, structure, and intended uses of buildings within those areas.

Zoning ordinance: The regulations and laws that control the use or improvement of land in a particular area or zone.

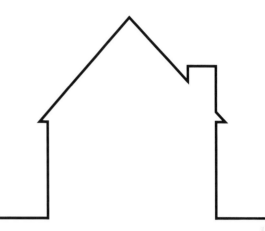

APPENDIX A
STANDARDIZED
TESTING COMPANIES

If your state uses one of these companies, contact them directly to obtain an information packet on the exam. Below is the contact information for these companies.

Applied Measurement Professionals
18000 W. 105th Street
Olathe, KS 66061-7543
www.goamp.com

Pearson Vue
Three Bala Plaza West, Suite 300
Bala Cynwyd, PA 19004
http://home.pearsonvue.com

Prometric
Canton Crossing
1501 South Clinton Street
Baltimore, MD 21224
866-PROMETRIC (776-6387)
443-455-8000
www.prometric.com

Psychological Services, Inc.
3210 East Tropicana
Las Vegas, NV 89121
800-733-9267
https://candidate.psiexams.com

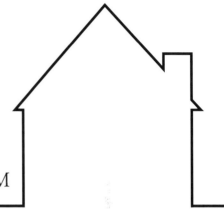

APPENDIX B

STATE-BY-STATE GUIDELINES FOR THE REAL ESTATE AGENT EXAM

To find the state-by-state guidelines for the real estate agent exam, navigate through **www.tests.com**.

For example, to see the guidelines for Alabama, the link is **www.tests.com/ Alabama-Real-Estate-Agent-Exam**.

From this webpage, there is a list of every state's guidelines in the panel on the right-hand side of the page. To find your state, simply click the corresponding link.

Another option is to browse through Mortgage News Daily's website at **www.mortgagenewsdaily.com/real_estate_license**. From this page, there is also a panel on the right-hand side of the page that presents every state.

APPENDIX C
STATE REAL ESTATE
COMMISSIONS & BUREAUS

Alabama Real Estate Commission
1201 Carmichael Way
Montgomery, AL 36106
(334) 242-5544
https://arec.alabama.gov

Alaska Real Estate Commission
Robert B. Atwood Building
550 West 7th Avenue #1500
Anchorage, AK 99501
(907) 269-8160
www.commerce.alaska.gov

Arizona Department of Real Estate
2910 N. 44th Street, Suite 100
Phoenix, AZ 85018
(602) 771 7799
www.re.state.az.us

Arkansas Real Estate Commission
612 South Summit Street
Little Rock, AR 72201-4740
(501) 683-8010
www.arec.arkansas.gov

California Bureau of Real Estate
1651 Exposition Blvd.
Sacramento, CA 95815
1 (877) 373-4542
www.dre.ca.gov

Colorado Department of
Regulatory Agencies
Division of Real Estate
1560 Broadway, Suite 925
Denver, CO 80202
(303) 894-2166
www.colorado.gov

Connecticut Department of
Consumer Protection
Real Estate Division
165 Capital Avenue
Hartford, CT 06106-1630
(860) 713-6100
www.ct.gov

Delaware Real Estate Commission
Cannon Building, Suite 203
861 Silver Lake Blvd.
Dover, DE 19904
(302) 744-4500
www.dpr.delaware.gov

Florida Real Estate Commission
Department of Business and
Professional Regulation
1940 North Monroe Street
Tallahassee, FL 32399-1027
(850) 487-1395
www.myfloridalicense.com

Georgia Real Estate Commission
229 Peachtree Street, N.E.
International Tower, Suite 1000
Atlanta, GA 30303-1605
(404) 656-3916
www.grec.state.ga.us

Hawaii Department of Commerce
and Consumer Affairs
Real Estate Branch
King Kalakaua Building
335 Merchant Street, Rm 333
Honolulu, HI 96813
(808) 586-2643
http://cca.hawaii.gov

Idaho Real Estate Commission
575 E. Parkcenter Blvd. Suite 180
Boise, ID 83706
(208) 334-3285
http://irec.idaho.gov

Illinois Department of Financial
and Professional Regulation
Division of Real Estate
320 West Washington Street, 3rd
Floor
Springfield, IL 62786
1 (888) 473-4858
www.idfpr.com
Note: For Illinois, there is also a Chicago office. Visit the website for more information.

Professional Licensing Agency
Attn: Indiana Real Estate
Commission
402 W Washington Street, Room
W072
Indianapolis, IN 46204
www.in.gov

Professional Licensing Bureau
200 E Grand Ave #350
Des Moines, IA 50309
(515) 281-7393
http://plb.iowa.gov

Kansas Real Estate Commission
Three Townsite Plaza, Ste. 200
120 SE 6th Avenue
Topeka, KS 66603-3511
(785) 296-3411
www.kansas.gov

Kentucky Real Estate Commission
10200 Linn Station Read
Suite 201
Louisville, KY 40223
(502) 429-7250
http://krec.ky.gov

Louisiana Real Estate Commission
P.O. Box 14785
Baton Rouge, LA 70898-4785
(225) 925-1923
www.irec.state.la.us
*Note: The physical address differs
from the mailing address. Provided
here is the mailing address. See the
website for more information.*

Maine Department of Professional
and Financial Regulation
Office of Professional and
Occupational Registration
35 State House Station
Augusta, Maine 04333-0035
(207) 624-8603
www.maine.gov
*Note: The physical address differs
from the mailing address. Provided
here is the mailing address. See the
website for more information.*

Real Estate Commission
500 North Calvert Street
Baltimore, MD 21202
(410) 230-6200
www.dllr.state.md.us

Office of Consumer Affairs &
Business Regulation
Ten Park Plaza, Suite 5170
Boston, MA 02116
(617) 973-8700
www.mass.gov

Michigan Department of Licensing
and Regulatory Affairs
P.O. Box 30004
Lansing, MI 48909
(517) 373-1820
www.michigan.gov
*Note: The physical address differs
from the mailing address. Provided
here is the mailing address. See the
website for more information.*

Minnesota Department of
Commerce
85 7th Place East
St. Paul, MN 55101
(651) 539-1600
http://mn.gov

Mississippi Real Estate
Commission
P.O. Box 12685
Jackson, MS 39236
(601) 321-6970
www.mrec.ms.gov
*Note: The physical address differs
from the mailing address. Provided
here is the mailing address. See the
website for more information.*

Missouri Division of Professional
Registration
3605 Missouri Boulevard
P.O. Box 1335
Jefferson City, MO 65102-1335
(573) 751-0293
http://pr.mo.gov

Montana Board of Realty
Regulation
301 South Park, 4th Floor
P.O. Box 200513
Helena, MT 59620-0513
(406) 841-2202
http://bsd.dli.mt.gov

Nebraska Real Estate Commission
301 Centennial Mall South
P.O. Box 94667
Lincoln, NE 68509-4667
(402) 471-2004
www.nrec.ne.gov

Department of Business and Industry
Nevada Real Estate Division
2501 E. Sahara Ave, Suite 102
Las Vegas, Nevada 89104
(702) 486-4033
http://red.nv.gov
Note: There is a second office located in Carson City. For more information, visit the website.

NH Real Estate Commission
121 South Fruit Street
Concord, NH 03301-2412
(603) 271-2219
www.nh.gov

NJ Real Estate Commission
P.O. Box 328
Trenton, NJ 08625-0328
(609) 292-7272
www.nj.gov
Note: The physical address differs from the mailing address. Provided here is the mailing address. See the website for more information.

New Mexico Real Estate
Commission
5500 San Antonio Dr. NE Suite B
Albuquerque, New Mexico 87109
(505) 222-9820
www.rld.state.nm.us

Department of State
Division of Licensing Services
One Commerce Plaza, 99
Washington Ave
Albany, NY 12231-0001
(518) 474-4429
www.dos.ny.gov

North Carolina Real Estate
Commission
P.O. Box 17100
Raleigh, NC 27619-7100
(919) 875-3700
www.ncrec.gov
Note: The physical address differs from the mailing address. Provided here is the mailing address. See the website for more information.

Real Estate Commission
P.O. Box 727
Bismarck, ND 58502-0727
www.realestatend.org
Note: The physical address differs from the mailing address. Provided here is the mailing address. See the website for more information.

Ohio Department of Commerce
Division of Real Estate and
Professional Licensing
77 South High Street, 20th Floor
Columbus, OH 43215-6133
(614) 466-4100
www.com.ohio.gov

Oklahoma Real Estate Commission
Denver N Davison Building
1915 N Stiles Ave, Suite 200
Oklahoma City, Oklahoma 73105
(405) 521-3387
www.ok.gov

Oregon Real Estate Agency
530 Center St NE Ste 100
Salem, OR 97301-3740
(503) 378-4170
www.oregon.gov

State Real Estate Commission
P.O. Box 2649
Harrisburg, PA 17105-2649
(717) 783-3658
www.dos.pa.gov
Note: The physical address differs from the mailing address. Provided here is the mailing address. See the website for more information.

Rhode Island Department of
Business Regulation
Division of Commercial Licensing
and Regulation Real Estate
1511 Pontiac Avenue
Cranston, RI 02920
(401) 462-9500
www.dbr.state.ri.us

South Carolina Department of
Labor Licensing and Regulation
Real Estate Commission
P.O. Box 11329
Columbia, SC 29211
(803) 896-4300
www.llronline.com
Note: The physical address differs from the mailing address. Provided here is the mailing address. See the website for more information.

South Dakota Real Estate
Commission
221 W. Capital, Suite 101
Pierre, SD 57501
(605) 773-3600
http://dlr.sd.gov

Tennessee Department of
Commerce & Insurance
Real Estate Commission
500 James Robertson Parkway
Davy Crockett Tower
Nashville, TN 37243-0565
(615) 741-2241
www.tn.gov

Texas Real Estate Commission
P.O. Box 12188
Austin, TX 78711-2188
(512) 936-3000
www.trec.state.tx.us
*Note: The physical address differs
from the mailing address. Provided
here is the mailing address. See the
website for more information.*

Utah Division of Real Estate
P.O. Box 146711
Salt Lake City, UT 84114-6711
(801) 530-6747
http://realestate.utah.gov
*Note: The physical address differs
from the mailing address. Provided
here is the mailing address. See the
website for more information.*

Vermont Office of Professional
Regulation
128 State Street
Montpelier, VT 05633-1101
(802) 828-2363
www.sec.state.vt.us

Department of Professional and
Occupational Regulation
9960 Mayland Drive
Suite 400
Richmond, VA 23233-1485
(804) 367-8526
www.dpor.virginia.gov

Washington Real Estate Licensing
Department of Licensing
PO Box 3917
Seattle, WA 98124-3917
(360) 664-6488
www.dol.wa.gov
*Note: The physical address differs
from the mailing address. Provided
here is the mailing address. See the
website for more information.*

West Virginia Real Estate
Commission
300 Capitol Street, Suite 400
Charleston, WV 25301
(304) 558-3555
www.wvrec.org

State of Wisconson
Department of Safety and
Professional Services
P.O. Box 8935
Madison, WI 53708-8935
(608) 266-2112
http://dsps.wi.gov
*Note: The physical address differs
from the mailing address. Provided
here is the mailing address. See the
website for more information.*

Real Estate Commission
2617 E. Lincolnway, Suite H
Cheyenne, WY 82002
(307) 777-7141
http://realestate.wyo.gov

APPENDIX D

UNIFORM APPRAISAL REPORT

Uniform Residential Appraisal Report   File

The purpose of this summary appraisal report is to provide the lender/client with an accurate, and adequately supported, opinion of the market value of the subject property.

Property Address	City	State	Zip Code
Borrower	Owner of Public Record	County	
Legal Description			
Assessor's Parcel #	Tax Year	R.E. Taxes $	
Neighborhood Name	Map Reference	Census Tract	

Occupant ☐ Owner ☐ Tenant ☐ Vacant   Special Assessments $ ☐ PUD   HOA $ ☐ per year ☐ per month

Property Rights Appraised ☐ Fee Simple ☐ Leasehold ☐ Other (describe)

Assignment Type ☐ Purchase Transaction ☐ Refinance Transaction ☐ Other (describe)

Lender/Client   Address

Is the subject property currently offered for sale or has it been offered for sale in the twelve months prior to the effective date of this appraisal? ☐ Yes ☐ No

Report data source(s) used, offering price(s), and date(s).

CONTRACT

I ☐ did ☐ did not analyze the contract for sale for the subject purchase transaction. Explain the results of the analysis of the contract for sale or why the analysis was not performed.

Contract Price $ Date of Contract   Is the property seller the owner of public record? ☐ Yes ☐ No Data Source(s)

Is there any financial assistance (loan charges, sale concessions, gift or downpayment assistance, etc.) to be paid by any party on behalf of the borrower? ☐ Yes ☐ No

If Yes, report the total dollar amount and describe the items to be paid.

NEIGHBORHOOD

Note: Race and the racial composition of the neighborhood are not appraisal factors.

Neighborhood Characteristics			One-Unit Housing Trends			One-Unit Housing		Present Land Use %	
Location ☐ Urban ☐ Suburban ☐ Rural			Property Values ☐ Increasing ☐ Stable ☐ Declining			PRICE	AGE	One-Unit	%
Built-Up ☐ Over 75% ☐ 25–75% ☐ Under 25%			Demand/Supply ☐ Shortage ☐ In Balance ☐ Over Supply			$ (000)	(yrs)	2-4 Unit	%
Growth ☐ Rapid ☐ Stable ☐ Slow			Marketing Time ☐ Under 3 mths ☐ 3-6 mths ☐ Over 6 mths			Low		Multi-Family	%
Neighborhood Boundaries						High		Commercial	%
						Pred.		Other	%

Neighborhood Description

Market Conditions (including support for the above conclusions)

SITE

Dimensions	Area	Shape	View
Specific Zoning Classification	Zoning Description		

Zoning Compliance ☐ Legal ☐ Legal Nonconforming (Grandfathered Use) ☐ No Zoning ☐ Illegal (describe)

Is the highest and best use of the subject property as improved (or as proposed per plans and specifications) the present use? ☐ Yes ☐ No If No, describe

Utilities Public Other (describe)		Public Other (describe)		Off-site Improvements—Type	Public	Private
Electricity ☐ ☐	Water ☐ ☐			Street	☐	☐
Gas ☐ ☐	Sanitary Sewer ☐ ☐			Alley	☐	☐

FEMA Special Flood Hazard Area ☐ Yes ☐ No FEMA Flood Zone   FEMA Map #   FEMA Map Date

Are the utilities and off-site improvements typical for the market area? ☐ Yes ☐ No If No, describe

Are there any adverse site conditions or external factors (easements, encroachments, environmental conditions, land uses, etc.)? ☐ Yes ☐ No If Yes, describe

IMPROVEMENTS

General Description		Foundation		Exterior Description materials/condition	Interior materials/condition	
Units ☐ One ☐ One with Accessory Unit		☐ Concrete Slab ☐ Crawl Space		Foundation Walls	Floors	
# of Stories		☐ Full Basement ☐ Partial Basement		Exterior Walls	Walls	
Type ☐ Det. ☐ Att. ☐ S-Det./End Unit		Basement Area sq. ft.		Roof Surface	Trim/Finish	
☐ Existing ☐ Proposed ☐ Under Const.		Basement Finish %		Gutters & Downspouts	Bath Floor	
Design (Style)		☐ Outside Entry/Exit ☐ Sump Pump		Window Type	Bath Wainscot	
Year Built		Evidence of ☐ Infestation		Storm Sash/Insulated	Car Storage ☐ None	
Effective Age (Yrs)		☐ Dampness ☐ Settlement		Screens	☐ Driveway # of Cars	
Attic ☐ None		Heating ☐ FWA ☐ HWBB ☐ Radiant	Amenities	☐ Woodstove(s) #	Driveway Surface	
☐ Drop Stair ☐ Stairs		☐ Other Fuel	☐ Fireplace(s) #	☐ Fence	☐ Garage # of Cars	
☐ Floor ☐ Scuttle		Cooling ☐ Central Air Conditioning	☐ Patio/Deck	☐ Porch	☐ Carport # of Cars	
☐ Finished ☐ Heated		☐ Individual ☐ Other	☐ Pool	☐ Other	☐ Att. ☐ Det. ☐ Built-in	

Appliances ☐ Refrigerator ☐ Range/Oven ☐ Dishwasher ☐ Disposal ☐ Microwave ☐ Washer/Dryer ☐ Other (describe)

Finished area above grade contains: Rooms   Bedrooms   Bath(s)   Square Feet of Gross Living Area Above Grade

Additional features (special energy efficient items, etc.)

Describe the condition of the property (including needed repairs, deterioration, renovations, remodeling, etc.)

Are there any physical deficiencies or adverse conditions that affect the livability, soundness, or structural integrity of the property? ☐ Yes ☐ No If Yes, describe

Does the property generally conform to the neighborhood (functional utility, style, condition, use, construction, etc.)? ☐ Yes ☐ No If No, describe

Uniform Residential Appraisal Report

File #

There are comparable properties currently offered for sale in the subject neighborhood ranging in price from $ to $

There are comparable sales in the subject neighborhood within the past twelve months ranging in sale price from $ to $

SALES COMPARISON APPROACH

FEATURE	SUBJECT	COMPARABLE SALE # 1		COMPARABLE SALE # 2		COMPARABLE SALE # 3	
Address							
Proximity to Subject							
Sale Price	$		$		$		$
Sale Price/Gross Liv. Area	$ sq. ft.	$ sq. ft.		$ sq. ft.		$ sq. ft.	
Data Source(s)							
Verification Source(s)							
VALUE ADJUSTMENTS	DESCRIPTION	DESCRIPTION	+(-) $ Adjustment	DESCRIPTION	+(-) $ Adjustment	DESCRIPTION	+(-) $ Adjustment
Sale or Financing Concessions							
Date of Sale/Time							
Location							
Leasehold/Fee Simple							
Site							
View							
Design (Style)							
Quality of Construction							
Actual Age							
Condition							
Above Grade Room Count	Total / Bdrms. / Baths	Total / Bdrms. / Baths		Total / Bdrms. / Baths		Total / Bdrms. / Baths	
Gross Living Area	sq. ft.	sq. ft.		sq. ft.		sq. ft.	
Basement & Finished Rooms Below Grade							
Functional Utility							
Heating/Cooling							
Energy Efficient Items							
Garage/Carport							
Porch/Patio/Deck							
Net Adjustment (Total)		☐ + ☐ -	$	☐ + ☐ -	$	☐ + ☐ -	$
Adjusted Sale Price of Comparables		Net Adj. % Gross Adj. %	$	Net Adj. % Gross Adj. %	$	Net Adj. % Gross Adj. %	$

I ☐ did ☐ did not research the sale or transfer history of the subject property and comparable sales. If not, explain

My research ☐ did ☐ did not reveal any prior sales or transfers of the subject property for the three years prior to the effective date of this appraisal.

Data source(s)

My research ☐ did ☐ did not reveal any prior sales or transfers of the comparable sales for the year prior to the date of sale of the comparable sale.

Data source(s)

Report the results of the research and analysis of the prior sale or transfer history of the subject property and comparable sales (report additional prior sales on page 3).

ITEM	SUBJECT	COMPARABLE SALE # 1	COMPARABLE SALE # 2	COMPARABLE SALE # 3
Date of Prior Sale/Transfer				
Price of Prior Sale/Transfer				
Data Source(s)				
Effective Date of Data Source(s)				

Analysis of prior sale or transfer history of the subject property and comparable sales

Summary of Sales Comparison Approach

Indicated Value by Sales Comparison Approach $

RECONCILIATION

Indicated Value by: Sales Comparison Approach $ Cost Approach (if developed) $ Income Approach (if developed) $

This appraisal is made ☐ "as is", ☐ subject to completion per plans and specifications on the basis of a hypothetical condition that the improvements have been completed, ☐ subject to the following repairs or alterations on the basis of a hypothetical condition that the repairs or alterations have been completed, or ☐ subject to the following required inspection based on the extraordinary assumption that the condition or deficiency does not require alteration or repair:

Based on a complete visual inspection of the interior and exterior areas of the subject property, defined scope of work, statement of assumptions and limiting conditions, and appraiser's certification, my (our) opinion of the market value, as defined, of the real property that is the subject of this report is $, as of , which is the date of inspection and the effective date of this appraisal.

Freddie Mac Form 70 March 2005 Page 2 of 6 Fannie Mae Form 1004 March 2005

Uniform Residential Appraisal Report　　File

ADDITIONAL COMMENTS

COST APPROACH TO VALUE (not required by Fannie Mae)

Provide adequate information for the lender/client to replicate the below cost figures and calculations.

Support for the opinion of site value (summary of comparable land sales or other methods for estimating site value)

ESTIMATED ☐ REPRODUCTION OR ☐ REPLACEMENT COST NEW	OPINION OF SITE VALUE	= $
Source of cost data	Dwelling　　　　Sq. Ft. @ $	= $
Quality rating from cost service　　Effective date of cost data	Sq. Ft. @ $	= $
Comments on Cost Approach (gross living area calculations, depreciation, etc.)		
	Garage/Carport　　Sq. Ft. @ $	= $
	Total Estimate of Cost-New	= $
	Less　　Physical　Functional　External	
	Depreciation	= $( )
	Depreciated Cost of Improvements	= $
	"As-is" Value of Site Improvements	= $
Estimated Remaining Economic Life (HUD and VA only)　　Years	Indicated Value By Cost Approach	= $

INCOME APPROACH TO VALUE (not required by Fannie Mae)

Estimated Monthly Market Rent $　　X Gross Rent Multiplier　　= $　　Indicated Value by Income Approach

Summary of Income Approach (including support for market rent and GRM)

PROJECT INFORMATION FOR PUDs (if applicable)

Is the developer/builder in control of the Homeowners' Association (HOA)? ☐ Yes ☐ No　Unit type(s) ☐ Detached ☐ Attached

Provide the following information for PUDs ONLY if the developer/builder is in control of the HOA and the subject property is an attached dwelling unit.

Legal name of project

Total number of phases　　Total number of units　　Total number of units sold
Total number of units rented　　Total number of units for sale　　Data source(s)

Was the project created by the conversion of an existing building(s) into a PUD? ☐ Yes ☐ No　If Yes, date of conversion

Does the project contain any multi-dwelling units? ☐ Yes ☐ No　Data source(s)

Are the units, common elements, and recreation facilities complete? ☐ Yes ☐ No　If No, describe the status of completion.

Are the common elements leased to or by the Homeowners' Association? ☐ Yes ☐ No　If Yes, describe the rental terms and options.

Describe common elements and recreational facilities

Freddie Mac Form 70　March 2005　　　　Page 3 of 6　　　　Fannie Mae Form 1004　March 2005

Uniform Residential Appraisal Report

File #

This report form is designed to report an appraisal of a one-unit property or a one-unit property with an accessory unit; including a unit in a planned unit development (PUD). This report form is not designed to report an appraisal of a manufactured home or a unit in a condominium or cooperative project.

This appraisal report is subject to the following scope of work, intended use, intended user, definition of market value, statement of assumptions and limiting conditions, and certifications. Modifications, additions, or deletions to the intended use, intended user, definition of market value, or assumptions and limiting conditions are not permitted. The appraiser may expand the scope of work to include any additional research or analysis necessary based on the complexity of this appraisal assignment. Modifications or deletions to the certifications are also not permitted. However, additional certifications that do not constitute material alterations to this appraisal report, such as those required by law or those related to the appraiser's continuing education or membership in an appraisal organization, are permitted.

SCOPE OF WORK: The scope of work for this appraisal is defined by the complexity of this appraisal assignment and the reporting requirements of this appraisal report form, including the following definition of market value, statement of assumptions and limiting conditions, and certifications. The appraiser must, at a minimum: (1) perform a complete visual inspection of the interior and exterior areas of the subject property, (2) inspect the neighborhood, (3) inspect each of the comparable sales from at least the street, (4) research, verify, and analyze data from reliable public and/or private sources, and (5) report his or her analysis, opinions, and conclusions in this appraisal report.

INTENDED USE: The intended use of this appraisal report is for the lender/client to evaluate the property that is the subject of this appraisal for a mortgage finance transaction.

INTENDED USER: The intended user of this appraisal report is the lender/client.

DEFINITION OF MARKET VALUE: The most probable price which a property should bring in a competitive and open market under all conditions requisite to a fair sale, the buyer and seller, each acting prudently, knowledgeably and assuming the price is not affected by undue stimulus. Implicit in this definition is the consummation of a sale as of a specified date and the passing of title from seller to buyer under conditions whereby: (1) buyer and seller are typically motivated; (2) both parties are well informed or well advised, and each acting in what he or she considers his or her own best interest; (3) a reasonable time is allowed for exposure in the open market; (4) payment is made in terms of cash in U. S. dollars or in terms of financial arrangements comparable thereto; and (5) the price represents the normal consideration for the property sold unaffected by special or creative financing or sales concessions* granted by anyone associated with the sale.

*Adjustments to the comparables must be made for special or creative financing or sales concessions. No adjustments are necessary for those costs which are normally paid by sellers as a result of tradition or law in a market area; these costs are readily identifiable since the seller pays these costs in virtually all sales transactions. Special or creative financing adjustments can be made to the comparable property by comparisons to financing terms offered by a third party institutional lender that is not already involved in the property or transaction. Any adjustment should not be calculated on a mechanical dollar for dollar cost of the financing or concession but the dollar amount of any adjustment should approximate the market's reaction to the financing or concessions based on the appraiser's judgment.

STATEMENT OF ASSUMPTIONS AND LIMITING CONDITIONS: The appraiser's certification in this report is subject to the following assumptions and limiting conditions.

1. The appraiser will not be responsible for matters of a legal nature that affect either the property being appraised or the title to it, except for information that he or she became aware of during the research involved in performing this appraisal. The appraiser assumes that the title is good and marketable and will not render any opinions about the title.

2. The appraiser has provided a sketch in this appraisal report to show the approximate dimensions of the improvements. The sketch is included only to assist the reader in visualizing the property and understanding the appraiser's determination of its size.

3. The appraiser has examined the available flood maps that are provided by the Federal Emergency Management Agency (or other data sources) and has noted in this appraisal report whether any portion of the subject site is located in an identified Special Flood Hazard Area. Because the appraiser is not a surveyor, he or she makes no guarantees, express or implied, regarding this determination.

4. The appraiser will not give testimony or appear in court because he or she made an appraisal of the property in question, unless specific arrangements to do so have been made beforehand, or as otherwise required by law.

5. The appraiser has noted in this appraisal report any adverse conditions (such as needed repairs, deterioration, the presence of hazardous wastes, toxic substances, etc.) observed during the inspection of the subject property or that he or she became aware of during the research involved in performing this appraisal. Unless otherwise stated in this appraisal report, the appraiser has no knowledge of any hidden or unapparent physical deficiencies or adverse conditions of the property (such as, but not limited to, needed repairs, deterioration, the presence of hazardous wastes, toxic substances, adverse environmental conditions, etc.) that would make the property less valuable, and has assumed that there are no such conditions and makes no guarantees or warranties, express or implied. The appraiser will not be responsible for any such conditions that do exist or for any engineering or testing that might be required to discover whether such conditions exist. Because the appraiser is not an expert in the field of environmental hazards, this appraisal report must not be considered as an environmental assessment of the property.

6. The appraiser has based his or her appraisal report and valuation conclusion for an appraisal that is subject to satisfactory completion, repairs, or alterations on the assumption that the completion, repairs, or alterations of the subject property will be performed in a professional manner.

Uniform Residential Appraisal Report　　　File

APPRAISER'S CERTIFICATION: The Appraiser certifies and agrees that:

1. I have, at a minimum, developed and reported this appraisal in accordance with the scope of work requirements stated in this appraisal report.

2. I performed a complete visual inspection of the interior and exterior areas of the subject property. I reported the condition of the improvements in factual, specific terms. I identified and reported the physical deficiencies that could affect the livability, soundness, or structural integrity of the property.

3. I performed this appraisal in accordance with the requirements of the Uniform Standards of Professional Appraisal Practice that were adopted and promulgated by the Appraisal Standards Board of The Appraisal Foundation and that were in place at the time this appraisal report was prepared.

4. I developed my opinion of the market value of the real property that is the subject of this report based on the sales comparison approach to value. I have adequate comparable market data to develop a reliable sales comparison approach for this appraisal assignment. I further certify that I considered the cost and income approaches to value but did not develop them, unless otherwise indicated in this report.

5. I researched, verified, analyzed, and reported on any current agreement for sale for the subject property, any offering for sale of the subject property in the twelve months prior to the effective date of this appraisal, and the prior sales of the subject property for a minimum of three years prior to the effective date of this appraisal, unless otherwise indicated in this report.

6. I researched, verified, analyzed, and reported on the prior sales of the comparable sales for a minimum of one year prior to the date of sale of the comparable sale, unless otherwise indicated in this report.

7. I selected and used comparable sales that are locationally, physically, and functionally the most similar to the subject property.

8. I have not used comparable sales that were the result of combining a land sale with the contract purchase price of a home that has been built or will be built on the land.

9. I have reported adjustments to the comparable sales that reflect the market's reaction to the differences between the subject property and the comparable sales.

10. I verified, from a disinterested source, all information in this report that was provided by parties who have a financial interest in the sale or financing of the subject property.

11. I have knowledge and experience in appraising this type of property in this market area.

12. I am aware of, and have access to, the necessary and appropriate public and private data sources, such as multiple listing services, tax assessment records, public land records and other such data sources for the area in which the property is located.

13. I obtained the information, estimates, and opinions furnished by other parties and expressed in this appraisal report from reliable sources that I believe to be true and correct.

14. I have taken into consideration the factors that have an impact on value with respect to the subject neighborhood, subject property, and the proximity of the subject property to adverse influences in the development of my opinion of market value. I have noted in this appraisal report any adverse conditions (such as, but not limited to, needed repairs, deterioration, the presence of hazardous wastes, toxic substances, adverse environmental conditions, etc.) observed during the inspection of the subject property or that I became aware of during the research involved in performing this appraisal. I have considered these adverse conditions in my analysis of the property value, and have reported on the effect of the conditions on the value and marketability of the subject property.

15. I have not knowingly withheld any significant information from this appraisal report and, to the best of my knowledge, all statements and information in this appraisal report are true and correct.

16. I stated in this appraisal report my own personal, unbiased, and professional analysis, opinions, and conclusions, which are subject only to the assumptions and limiting conditions in this appraisal report.

17. I have no present or prospective interest in the property that is the subject of this report, and I have no present or prospective personal interest or bias with respect to the participants in the transaction. I did not base, either partially or completely, my analysis and/or opinion of market value in this appraisal report on the race, color, religion, sex, age, marital status, handicap, familial status, or national origin of either the prospective owners or occupants of the subject property or of the present owners or occupants of the properties in the vicinity of the subject property or on any other basis prohibited by law.

18. My employment and/or compensation for performing this appraisal or any future or anticipated appraisals was not conditioned on any agreement or understanding, written or otherwise, that I would report (or present analysis supporting) a predetermined specific value, a predetermined minimum value, a range or direction in value, a value that favors the cause of any party, or the attainment of a specific result or occurrence of a specific subsequent event (such as approval of a pending mortgage loan application).

19. I personally prepared all conclusions and opinions about the real estate that were set forth in this appraisal report. If I relied on significant real property appraisal assistance from any individual or individuals in the performance of this appraisal or the preparation of this appraisal report, I have named such individual(s) and disclosed the specific tasks performed in this appraisal report. I certify that any individual so named is qualified to perform the tasks. I have not authorized anyone to make a change to any item in this appraisal report; therefore, any change made to this appraisal is unauthorized and I will take no responsibility for it.

20. I identified the lender/client in this appraisal report who is the individual, organization, or agent for the organization that ordered and will receive this appraisal report.

Uniform Residential Appraisal Report

File #

21. The lender/client may disclose or distribute this appraisal report to: the borrower; another lender at the request of the borrower; the mortgagee or its successors and assigns; mortgage insurers; government sponsored enterprises; other secondary market participants; data collection or reporting services; professional appraisal organizations; any department, agency, or instrumentality of the United States; and any state, the District of Columbia, or other jurisdictions; without having to obtain the appraiser's or supervisory appraiser's (if applicable) consent. Such consent must be obtained before this appraisal report may be disclosed or distributed to any other party (including, but not limited to, the public through advertising, public relations, news, sales, or other media).

22. I am aware that any disclosure or distribution of this appraisal report by me or the lender/client may be subject to certain laws and regulations. Further, I am also subject to the provisions of the Uniform Standards of Professional Appraisal Practice that pertain to disclosure or distribution by me.

23. The borrower, another lender at the request of the borrower, the mortgagee or its successors and assigns, mortgage insurers, government sponsored enterprises, and other secondary market participants may rely on this appraisal report as part of any mortgage finance transaction that involves any one or more of these parties.

24. If this appraisal report was transmitted as an "electronic record" containing my "electronic signature," as those terms are defined in applicable federal and/or state laws (excluding audio and video recordings), or a facsimile transmission of this appraisal report containing a copy or representation of my signature, the appraisal report shall be as effective, enforceable and valid as if a paper version of this appraisal report were delivered containing my original hand written signature.

25. Any intentional or negligent misrepresentation(s) contained in this appraisal report may result in civil liability and/or criminal penalties including, but not limited to, fine or imprisonment or both under the provisions of Title 18, United States Code, Section 1001, et seq., or similar state laws.

SUPERVISORY APPRAISER'S CERTIFICATION: The Supervisory Appraiser certifies and agrees that:

1. I directly supervised the appraiser for this appraisal assignment, have read the appraisal report, and agree with the appraiser's analysis, opinions, statements, conclusions, and the appraiser's certification.

2. I accept full responsibility for the contents of this appraisal report including, but not limited to, the appraiser's analysis, opinions, statements, conclusions, and the appraiser's certification.

3. The appraiser identified in this appraisal report is either a sub-contractor or an employee of the supervisory appraiser (or the appraisal firm), is qualified to perform this appraisal, and is acceptable to perform this appraisal under the applicable state law.

4. This appraisal report complies with the Uniform Standards of Professional Appraisal Practice that were adopted and promulgated by the Appraisal Standards Board of The Appraisal Foundation and that were in place at the time this appraisal report was prepared.

5. If this appraisal report was transmitted as an "electronic record" containing my "electronic signature," as those terms are defined in applicable federal and/or state laws (excluding audio and video recordings), or a facsimile transmission of this appraisal report containing a copy or representation of my signature, the appraisal report shall be as effective, enforceable and valid as if a paper version of this appraisal report were delivered containing my original hand written signature.

APPRAISER

Signature_____
Name _____
Company Name _____
Company Address_____

Telephone Number _____
Email Address_____
Date of Signature and Report_____
Effective Date of Appraisal _____
State Certification #_____
or State License #_____
or Other (describe) _____ State # _____
State _____
Expiration Date of Certification or License _____

ADDRESS OF PROPERTY APPRAISED

_____
_____

APPRAISED VALUE OF SUBJECT PROPERTY $ _____
LENDER/CLIENT
Name _____
Company Name _____
Company Address_____
_____
Email Address_____

SUPERVISORY APPRAISER (ONLY IF REQUIRED)

Signature_____
Name_____
Company Name _____
Company Address_____
_____

Telephone Number _____
Email Address_____
Date of Signature _____
State Certification #_____
or State License # _____
State _____
Expiration Date of Certification or License _____

SUBJECT PROPERTY

☐ Did not inspect subject property
☐ Did inspect exterior of subject property from street
   Date of Inspection _____
☐ Did inspect interior and exterior of subject property
   Date of Inspection _____

COMPARABLE SALES

☐ Did not inspect exterior of comparable sales from street
☐ Did inspect exterior of comparable sales from street
   Date of Inspection _____

APPENDIX E

SAMPLE GOOD FAITH ESTIMATE

OMB Approval No. 2502-0265

Good Faith Estimate (GFE)

Name of Originator	Borrower
Originator Address	Property Address
Originator Phone Number	
Originator Email	Date of GFE

Purpose

This GFE gives you an estimate of your settlement charges and loan terms if you are approved for this loan. For more information, see HUD's *Special Information Booklet* on settlement charges, your *Truth-in-Lending Disclosures*, and other consumer information at www.hud.gov/respa. If you decide you would like to proceed with this loan, contact us.

Shopping for your loan

Only you can shop for the best loan for you. Compare this GFE with other loan offers, so you can find the best loan. Use the shopping chart on page 3 to compare all the offers you receive.

Important dates

1. The interest rate for this GFE is available through [   ]. After this time, the interest rate, some of your loan Origination Charges, and the monthly payment shown below can change until you lock your interest rate.

2. This estimate for all other settlement charges is available through [   ]

3. After you lock your interest rate, you must go to settlement within [   ] days (your rate lock period) to receive the locked interest rate.

4. You must lock the interest rate at least [   ] days before settlement.

Summary of your loan

Your initial loan amount is	$
Your loan term is	years
Your initial interest rate is	%
Your initial monthly amount owed for principal, interest, and any mortgage insurance is	$ per month
Can your interest rate rise?	☐ No ☐ Yes, it can rise to a maximum of %. The first change will be in
Even if you make payments on time, can your loan balance rise?	☐ No ☐ Yes, it can rise to a maximum of $
Even if you make payments on time, can your monthly amount owed for principal, interest, and any mortgage insurance rise?	☐ No ☐ Yes, the first increase can be in and the monthly amount owed can rise to $. The maximum it can ever rise to is $
Does your loan have a prepayment penalty?	☐ No ☐ Yes, your maximum prepayment penalty is $
Does your loan have a balloon payment?	☐ No ☐ Yes, you have a balloon payment of $ due in years.

Escrow account information

Some lenders require an escrow account to hold funds for paying property taxes or other property-related charges in addition to your monthly amount owed of $ [   ]
Do we require you to have an escrow account for your loan?
☐ No, you do not have an escrow account. You must pay these charges directly when due.
☐ Yes, you have an escrow account. It may or may not cover all of these charges. Ask us.

Summary of your settlement charges

A	Your Adjusted Origination Charges (See page 2.)	$
B	Your Charges for All Other Settlement Services (See page 2.)	$
A + **B**	Total Estimated Settlement Charges	$

Good Faith Estimate (HUD-GFE) 1

Understanding your estimated settlement charges

Your Adjusted Origination Charges

1. Our origination charge
This charge is for getting this loan for you.

2. Your credit or charge (points) for the specific interest rate chosen
- ☐ The credit or charge for the interest rate of [   ] % is included in "Our origination charge." (See item 1 above.)
- ☐ You receive a credit of $[   ] for this interest rate of [   ] %. This credit **reduces** your settlement charges.
- ☐ You pay a charge of $[   ] for this interest rate of [   ] %. This charge (points) **increases** your total settlement charges.

The tradeoff table on page 3 shows that you can change your total settlement charges by choosing a different interest rate for this loan.

A | Your Adjusted Origination Charges | $

Your Charges for All Other Settlement Services

Some of these charges can change at settlement. See the top of page 3 for more information.

3. Required services that we select
These charges are for services we require to complete your settlement. We will choose the providers of these services.

Service	Charge

4. Title services and lender's title insurance
This charge includes the services of a title or settlement agent, for example, and title insurance to protect the lender, if required.

5. Owner's title insurance
You may purchase an owner's title insurance policy to protect your interest in the property.

6. Required services that you can shop for
These charges are for other services that are required to complete your settlement. We can identify providers of these services or you can shop for them yourself. Our estimates for providing these services are below.

Service	Charge

7. Government recording charges
These charges are for state and local fees to record your loan and title documents.

8. Transfer taxes
These charges are for state and local fees on mortgages and home sales.

9. Initial deposit for your escrow account
This charge is held in an escrow account to pay future recurring charges on your property and includes ☐ all property taxes, ☐ all insurance, and ☐ other [   ]

10. Daily interest charges
This charge is for the daily interest on your loan from the day of your settlement until the first day of the next month or the first day of your normal mortgage payment cycle. This amount is $[   ] per day for [   ] days (if your settlement is [   ]).

11. Homeowner's insurance
This charge is for the insurance you must buy for the property to protect from a loss, such as fire.

Policy	Charge

B | Your Charges for All Other Settlement Services | $

A + **B** | Total Estimated Settlement Charges | $

 Good Faith Estimate (HUD-GFE) 2

Instructions

Understanding which charges can change at settlement

This GFE estimates your settlement charges. At your settlement, you will receive a HUD-1, a form that lists your actual costs. Compare the charges on the HUD-1 with the charges on this GFE. Charges can change if you select your own provider and do not use the companies we identify. (See below for details.)

These charges **cannot increase** at settlement:	The total of these charges **can increase up to 10%** at settlement:	These charges **can change** at settlement:
▪ Our origination charge ▪ Your credit or charge (points) for the specific interest rate chosen (after you lock in your interest rate) ▪ Your adjusted origination charges (after you lock in your interest rate) ▪ Transfer taxes	▪ Required services that we select ▪ Title services and lender's title insurance (if we select them or you use companies we identify) ▪ Owner's title insurance (if you use companies we identify) ▪ Required services that you can shop for (if you use companies we identify) ▪ Government recording charges	▪ Required services that you can shop for (if you do not use companies we identify) ▪ Title services and lender's title insurance (if you do not use companies we identify) ▪ Owner's title insurance (if you do not use companies we identify) ▪ Initial deposit for your escrow account ▪ Daily interest charges ▪ Homeowner's insurance

Using the tradeoff table

In this GFE, we offered you this loan with a particular interest rate and estimated settlement charges. However:
- If you want to choose this same loan with **lower settlement charges**, then you will have a **higher interest rate**.
- If you want to choose this same loan with a **lower interest rate**, then you will have **higher settlement charges**.

If you would like to choose an available option, you must ask us for a new GFE.

Loan originators have the option to complete this table. Please ask for additional information if the table is not completed.

	The loan in this GFE	The same loan with lower settlement charges	The same loan with a lower interest rate
Your initial loan amount	$	$	$
Your initial interest rate¹	%	%	%
Your initial monthly amount owed	$	$	$
Change in the monthly amount owed from this GFE	No change	You will pay $ **more** every month	You will pay $ **less** every month
Change in the amount you will pay at settlement with this interest rate	No change	Your settlement charges will be **reduced** by $	Your settlement charges will **increase** by $
How much your total estimated settlement charges will be	$	$	$

¹ For an adjustable rate loan, the comparisons above are for the initial interest rate before adjustments are made.

Using the shopping chart

Use this chart to compare GFEs from different loan originators. Fill in the information by using a different column for each GFE you receive. By comparing loan offers, you can shop for the best loan.

	This loan	Loan 2	Loan 3	Loan 4
Loan originator name				
Initial loan amount				
Loan term				
Initial interest rate				
Initial monthly amount owed				
Rate lock period				
Can interest rate rise?				
Can loan balance rise?				
Can monthly amount owed rise?				
Prepayment penalty?				
Balloon payment?				
Total Estimated Settlement Charges				

If your loan is sold in the future

Some lenders may sell your loan after settlement. Any fees lenders receive in the future cannot change the loan you receive or the charges you paid at settlement.

 Good Faith Estimate (HUD-GFE) 3

APPENDIX F

ACRONYMS

ACM: Asbestos Containing Materials

ADA: Americans with Disabilities Act

APR: Annual Percentage Rate

ARM: Adjustable-Rate Mortgages

AVM: Automated Valuation Model

BPO: Broker Price Opinion

CAM: Common Area Maintenance

CBA: Controlled Business Arrangement

CLO: Computerized Loan Origination

CMA: Comparative/Competitive Market Analysis

CO: Certificate of Occupancy

CPA: Certified Public Accountant

CPI: Consumer Price Index

CTC: Clear to Close

DBA: Doing Business As

DTI: Debt-to-Income Ratio

EPA: Environmental Protection Agency

FCRA: Fair Credit Reporting Act

FDIC: Federal Deposit Insurance Corporation

FEMA: Federal Emergency Management Agency

FHA: Federal Housing Administration (not to be confused with the Federal Housing Authority)

FHLMC: Federal Home Loan Mortgage Corporation

FNMA: Federal National Mortgage Association

FSBO: For Sale By Owner

GFE: Good Faith Estimate

GNMA: Government National Mortgage Association

GRI: Graduate, REALTOR® Institute

GRM: Gross Rent Multiplier

HECM: Home Equity Conversion Mortgage

HELOC: Home Equity Lines of Credit

HER: Housing Expense Ratio

HOA: Homeowners Association

HUD: Department of Housing and Urban Development

HVAC: Heating, Ventilating, and Air Conditioning

IBC: International Building Code

LCD: Lowest Common Denominator

LIBOR: London InterBank Offered Rate

LTV: Loan-to-Value Ratio

MGIC: Mortgage Guaranty Insurance Corporation

MI: Mortgage Insurance

MIP: Mortgage Insurance Premium

MLS: Multiple Listing Service

NAR: National Association of REALTORS®

NNN: Net lease, or triple net lease

NOI: Net Operating Income

P&I: Principal and Interest

P&S Agreement: Purchase and Sale Agreement

PITI: Principal, Interest, Taxes, Insurance

PMI: Private Mortgage Insurance

POC: Paid Outside Closing

PUD: Planned Unit Development

REIT: Real Estate Investment Trust

REO: Real Estate Owned

RESPA: Real Estate Settlement Procedures Act

RFP: Request for Proposal

ROI: Return on Investment

TI: Tenant Improvement

TILA: Truth in Lending Act

TSO: Timeshare Ownership Plan

URAR: Uniform Residential Appraisal Report

VA: Department of Veterans Affairs

VOD: Verification of Deposit

VOE: Verification of Employment

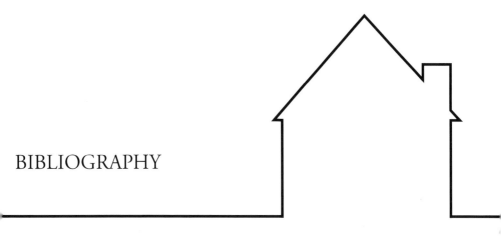

BIBLIOGRAPHY

"Assessing Civil Penalties for Fair Housing Act Cases." *Legal Information Institute*. Cornell University, 18 Jan. 2013. Web. 29 Jan. 2016.

"US Existing Single-Family Home Median Sales Price: November 2015." YCharts, 2015. Web. 29 Jan. 2016.

Gleason, Laura. "The New Dollar Threshold for Regulation Z Coverage." *Consumer Compliance Outlook*. Federal Reserve System, 2011. Web. 29 Jan. 2016.

www.homequitybuilder.info. Brentwood, NH: Ken Lambert Mortgage Enterprises LLC, 2008.

James Peter Regan. *Massachusetts Real Estate Principles and Practices*. Melrose, MA: North Shore Press, 2004. Print.

Real Estate Sales Exam. 2nd ed. New York: Learning Express LLC, 2007. Print.

www.myfloridalicense.com/dbpr/re/index.html, 2015

www.realestatelicensing.net/FAQ.php, 2016

Zibel, Alan, and Annamaria Andriotis. "Lenders Step Up Financing to Subprime Borrowers." *WSJ*. Dow Jones & Company, 18 Feb. 2015. Web. 29 Jan. 2016.

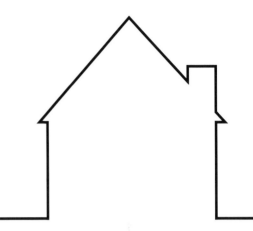

INDEX